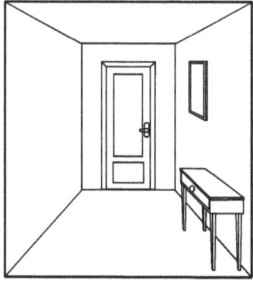

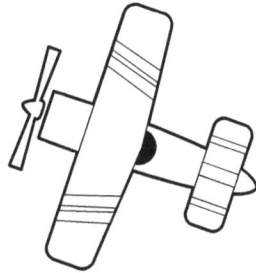

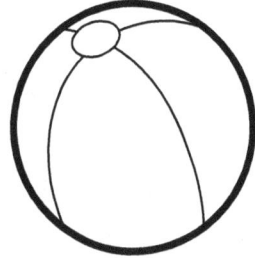

This Book Belongs To:

_____

DEAR PARENTS AND TEACHERS

Thank you for purchasing *My Favorite Toddler Coloring Book*! This book is a tool to help your child learn to focus as they develop and refine their motor skills and learn rudimentary concepts like the alphabet, numbers 1 through 10, counting, and pairing letters with objects.

Why Choose Coloring?

While on its surface it may seem simple, coloring regularly provides additional benefits for children entering or still in the early stages of the school system: they'll learn color recognition, improve their hand-eye coordination, and develop better handwriting.

Not only will more precise handwriting assist them in school, but their coloring sessions will also closely mirror activity sessions they'll share with other students in their class. This familiarity will make it easier for them to settle in and focus on their classroom activities.

What Makes This Coloring Book Stand Out?

In addition to being a coloring book, *My Favorite Toddler Coloring Book* features five sections teaching the following lessons:

- Numbers 1 Through 10
- Counting Objects
- Letters A Through Z
- Shapes
- Counting Shapes

Best of all, *My Favorite Toddler Coloring Book* is filled with objects and characters like Andy Ant your child will recognize from our Alphabet Series! By combining activities with our stories, we've created a more engaging experience your child will enjoy, full of learning opportunities as they connect characters and objects with the stories they belong to, strengthening their memory recall.

HOW TO USE THIS BOOK

My Favorite Toddler Coloring Book serves a dual purpose when used alongside the stories from our Alphabet Series. It provides the many benefits of coloring, and it also reinforces the lessons from each book!

Reintroduce your child to the new characters and returning faces found within the volume as they work their way through the book. Can they tell you the name of the object or character? Do they remember what the object is for or what the character did in the story?

These coloring pages are an excellent prompt to reopen our Alphabet Series books and experience their story all over again. Each letter will offer new opportunities for your child to learn to better link images and words within their memory.

You can find the name of the story that each illustration comes from at the bottom of its page. While we encourage pairing *My Favorite Toddler Coloring Book* with our Alphabet Series books, it also functions perfectly well as just a a coloring book. You don't need to own any of the storybooks for your child to enjoy hours of productive entertainment from these pages alone.

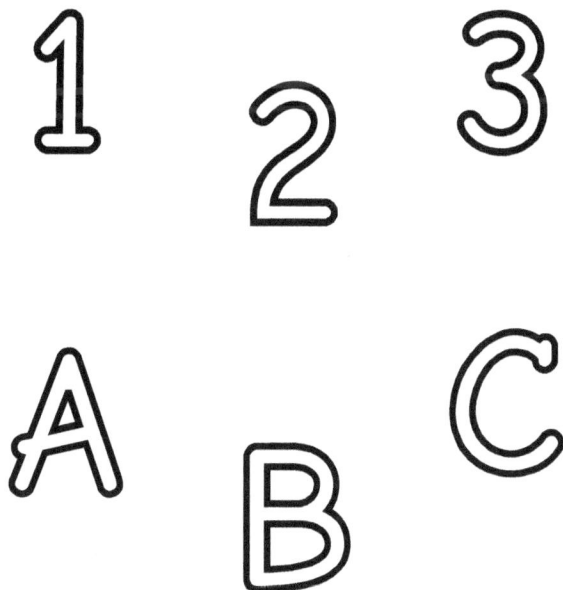

TEACH THE ALPHABET

A Complete Story Based Alphabet Curriculum!

Includes TWENTY SIX units - 26 weeks of preschool!

620+ Pages of DONE-FOR-YOU Planning!

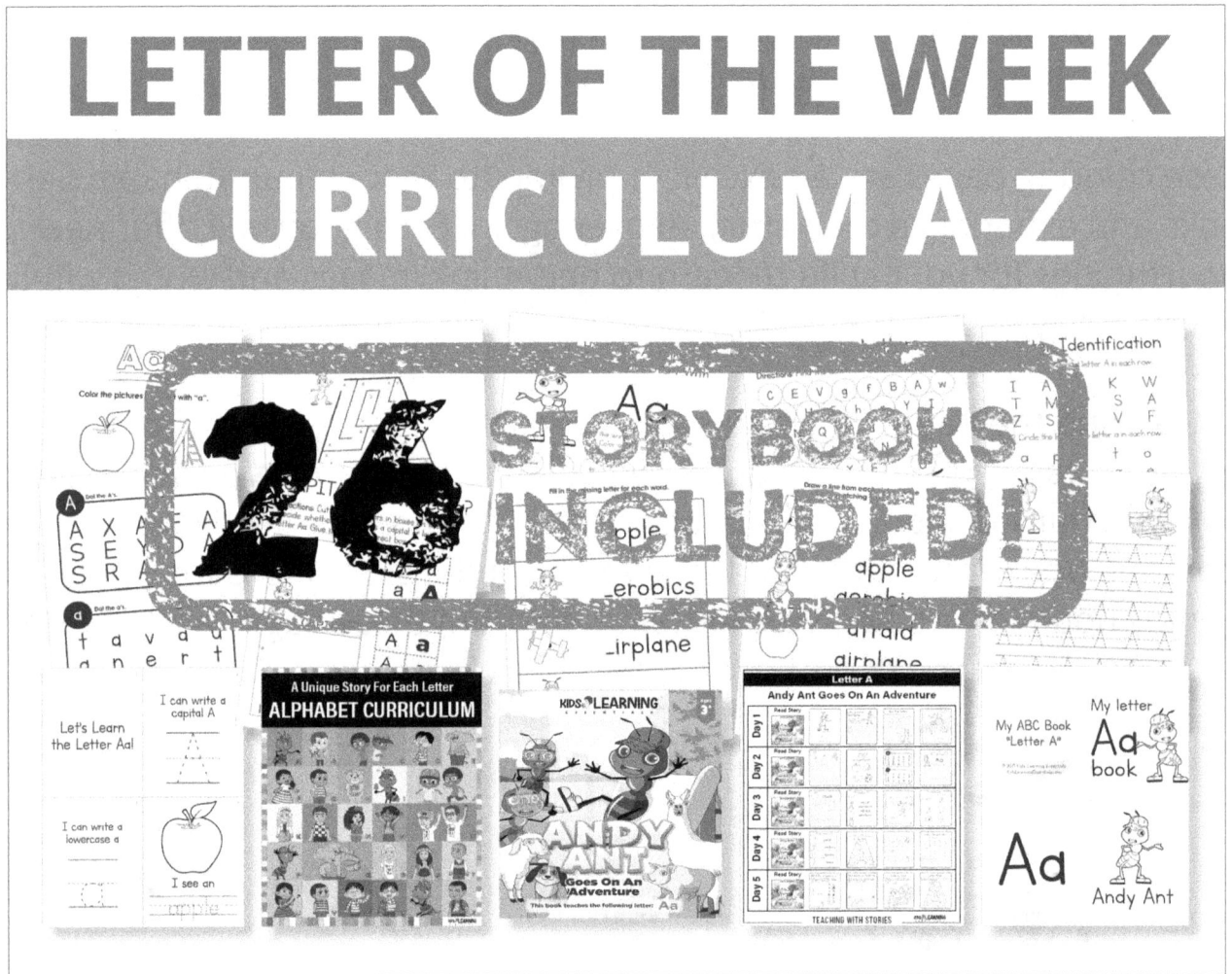

LETTER OF THE WEEK
CURRICULUM A-Z

26 STORYBOOKS INCLUDED!

A Unique Story For Each Letter
ALPHABET CURRICULUM

KIDS LEARNING

ANDY ANT Goes On An Adventure

Letter A
Andy Ant Goes On An Adventure

My ABC Book "Letter A"

My letter Aa book

Aa

Andy Ant

You can learn more by visiting the following link:
https://klelinks.com/alphabet-curriculum

FREE LETTER A LESSON PLAN

We've put together a lesson plan chock full of DONE-FOR-YOU planning with a **week** of activities to teach your child the letter A!

Everything you need to teach the letter A in one lesson plan.

Just download and print, and you're on your way!

FREE *Letter A Lesson Plan*

KIDS LEARNING   STORE.KIDSLEARNINGESSENTIALS.COM

You can learn more by visiting the following link:
https://klelinks.com/free-lesson-plan

FREE LETTER A FINGER PUPPETS

Finger puppets make for an excellent teaching method that combines both practicality and fun.

Children learn best when they're engaged, so we've provided the finger puppets for "Andy Ant Goes On An Adventure" for **FREE!**

You can learn more by visiting the following link:
https://klelinks.com/free-finger-puppets

FREE LETTER A CLOTHESLINE PUPPETS

Puppets make for an excellent teaching method that combines both practicality and fun.

To help your child feel more engaged with the story, we've provided the clothespin puppets accompanying "Andy Ant Goes On An Adventure" for **FREE!**

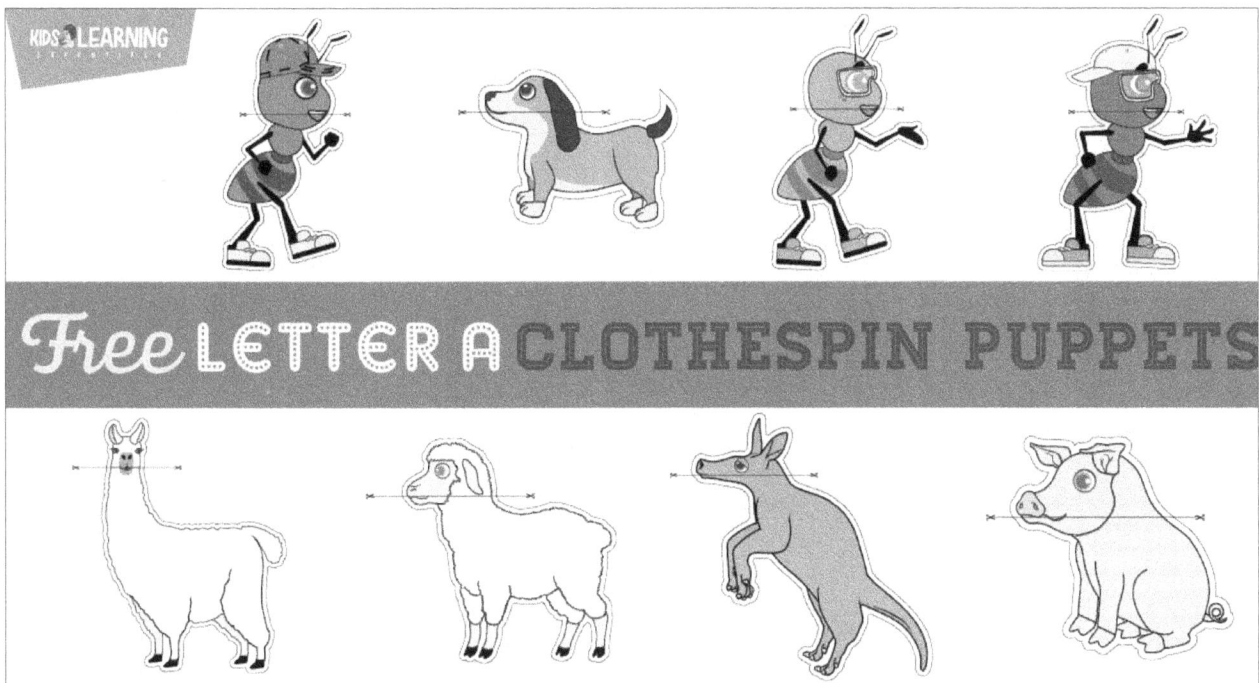

You can learn more by visiting the following link:
https://klelinks.com/free-clothespin-puppets

NUMBERS

1

3

2

1

ONE

2

TWO

3

THREE

4

FOUR

5

FIVE

6

SIX

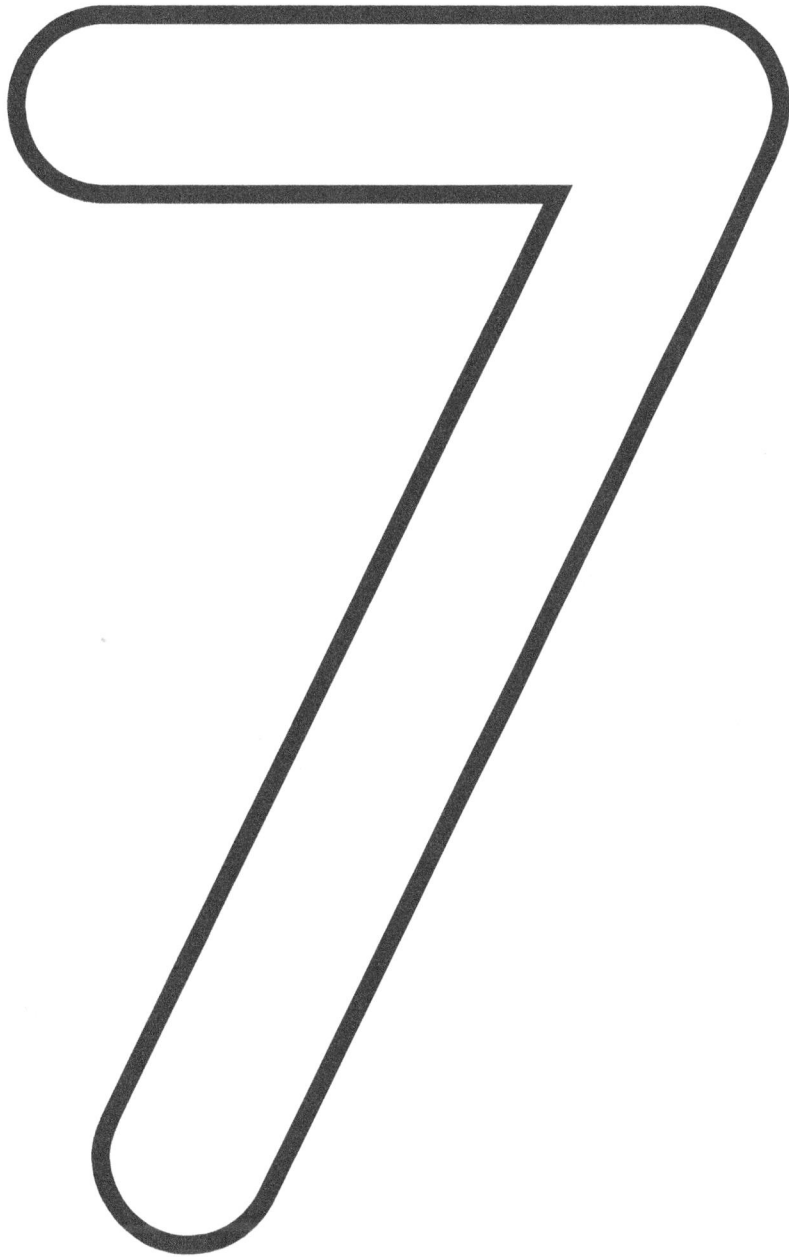

7

SEVEN

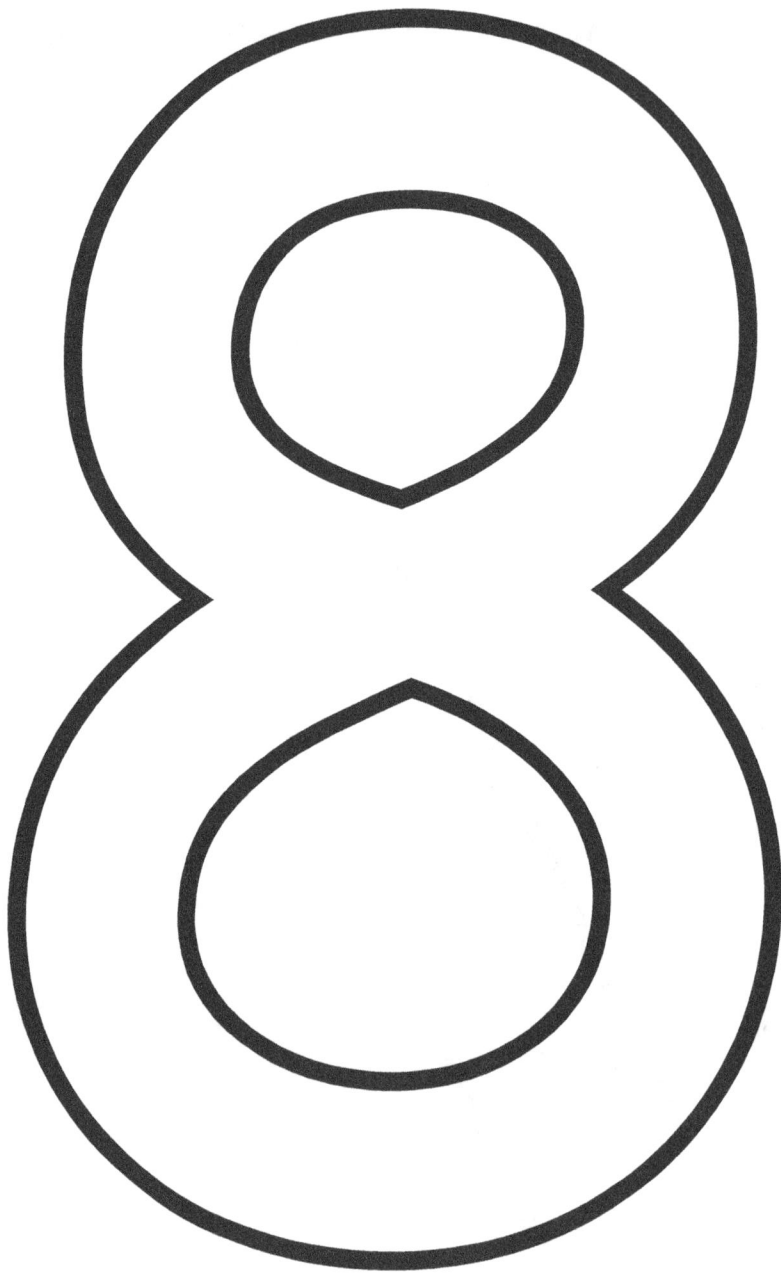

8

EIGHT

9

NINE

10

TEN

COUNTING OBJECTS

1   3

2

1

2

3

4

5

7

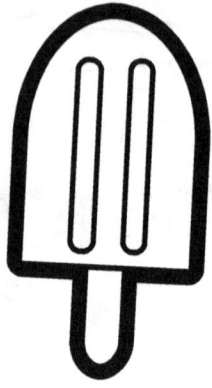

9

10

LETTERS

A
B
C
D

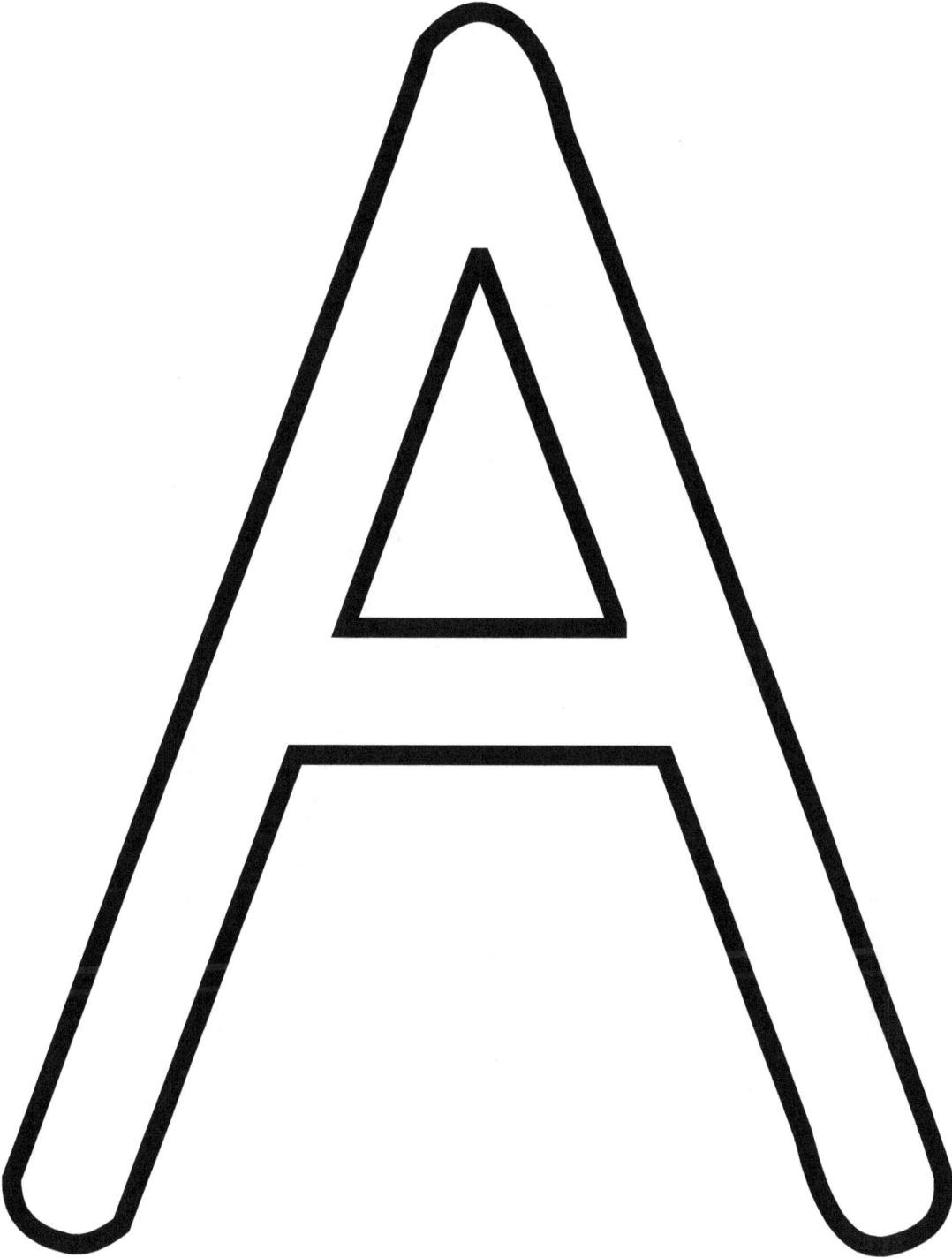

B

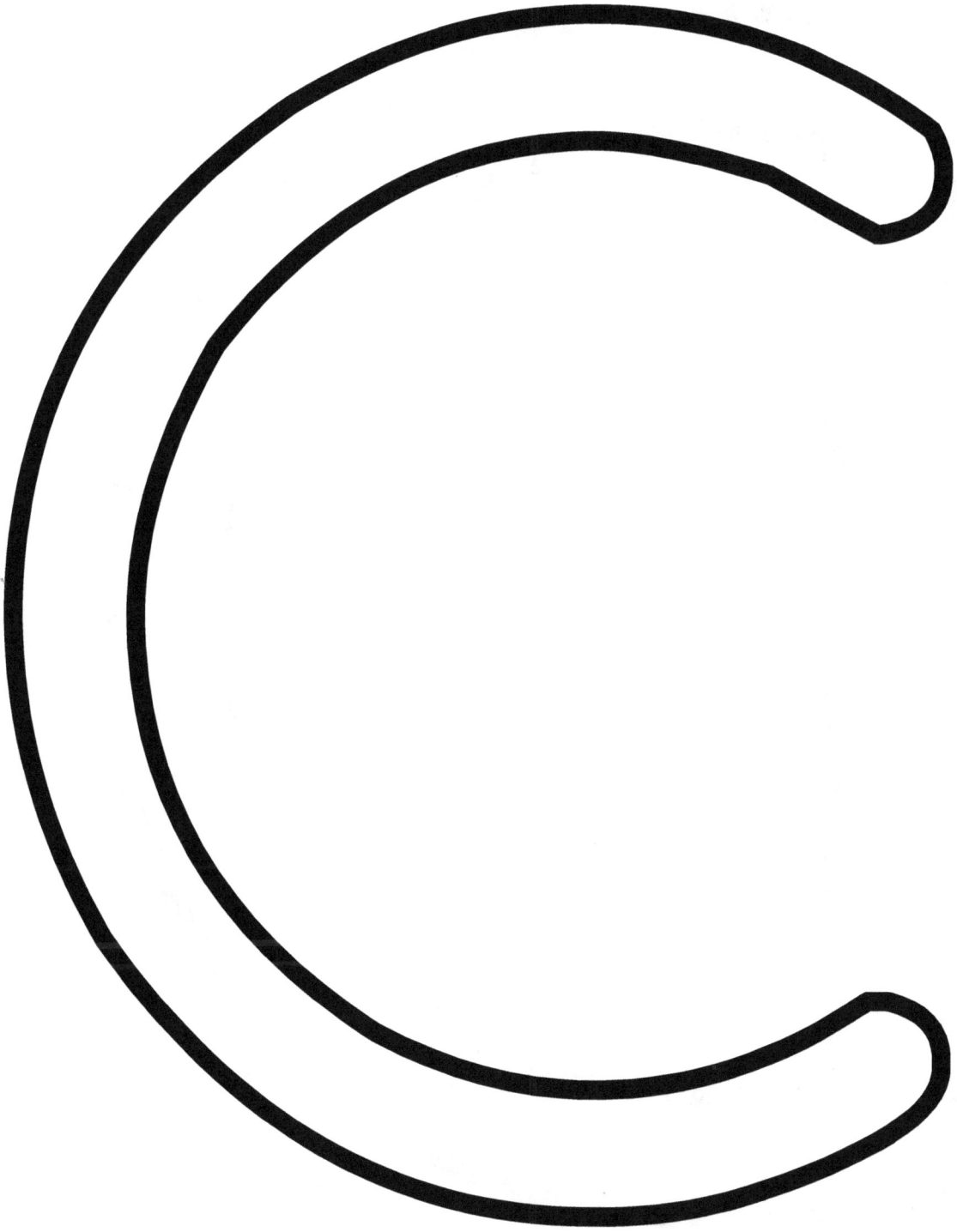

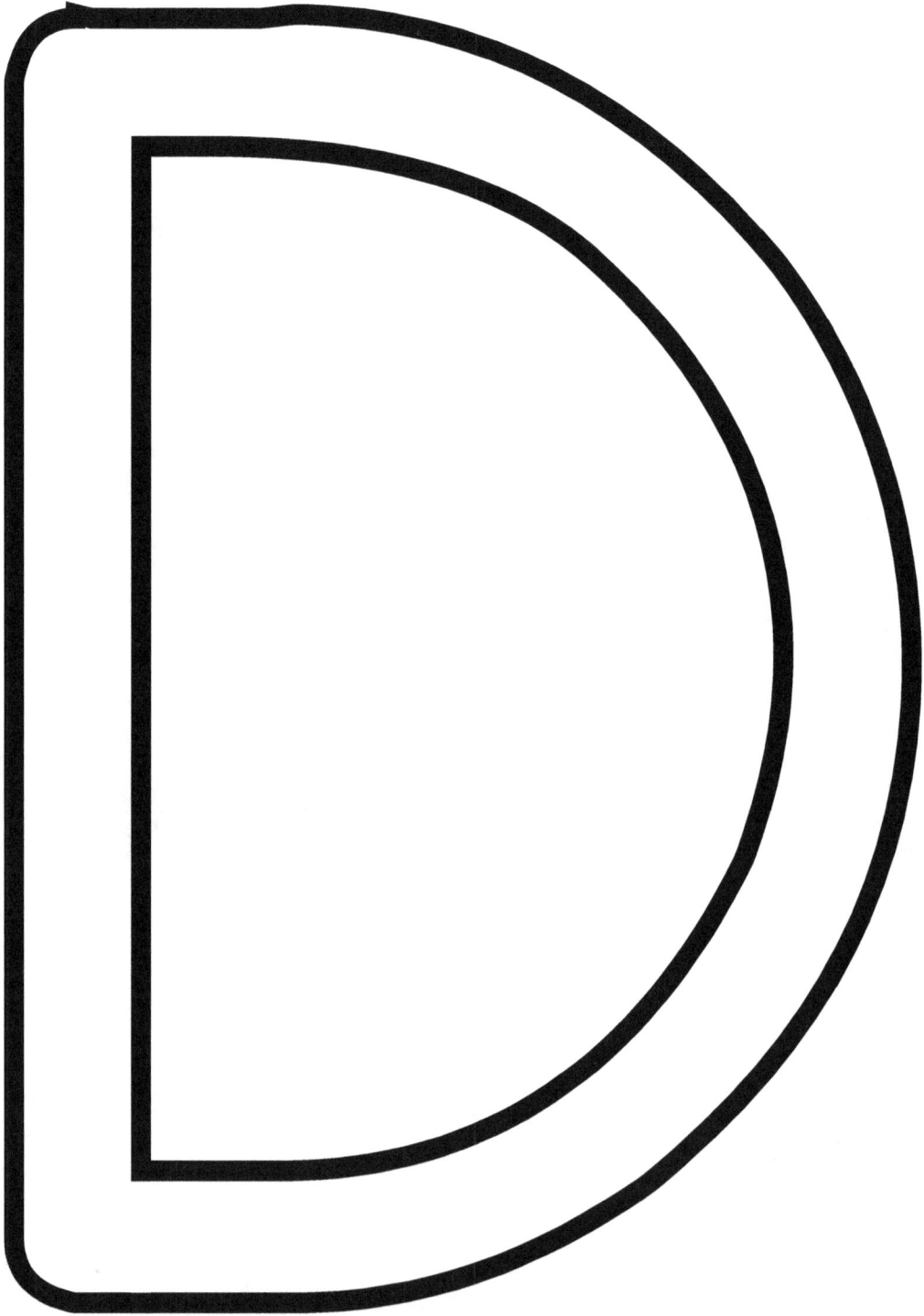

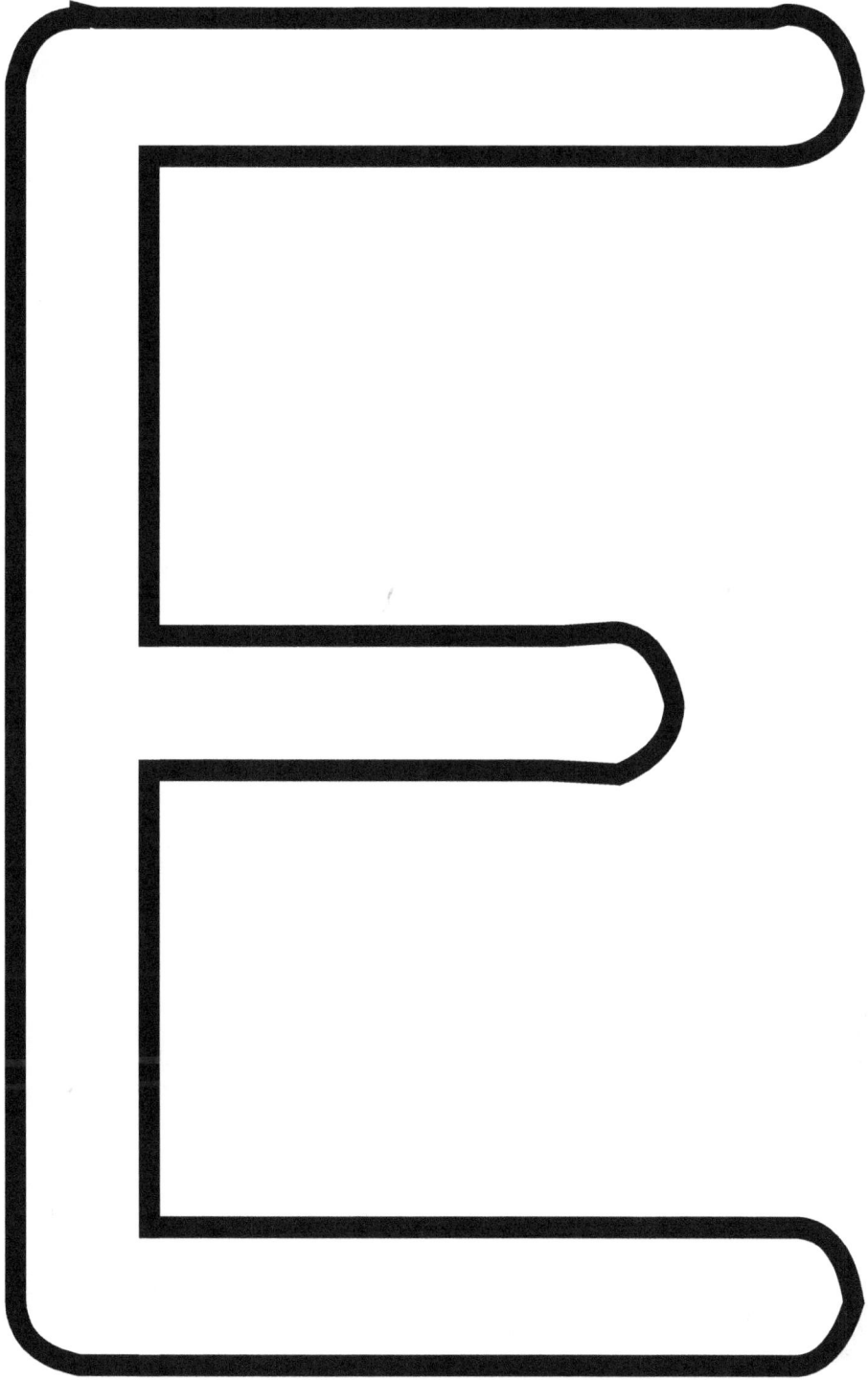

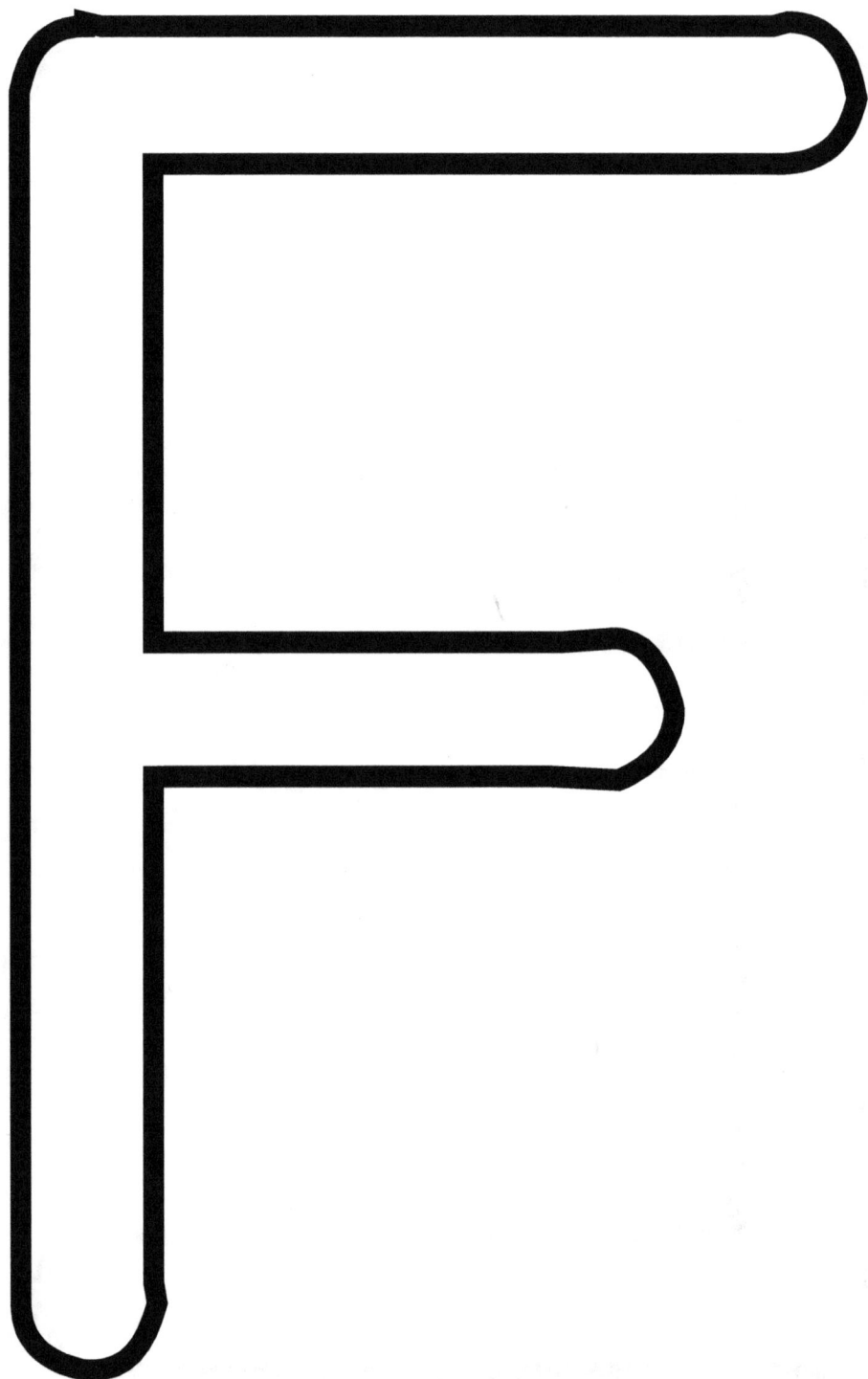

G

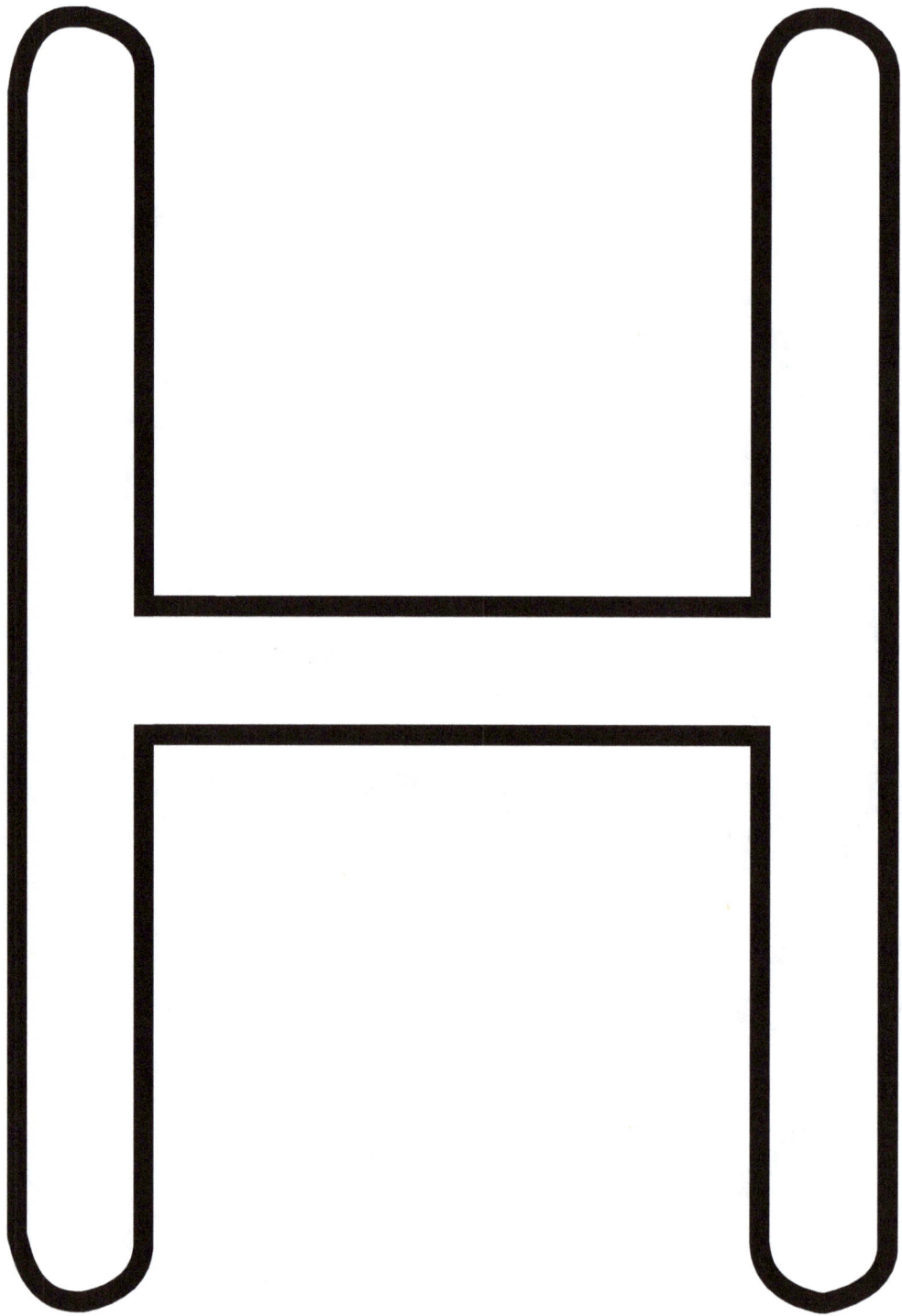

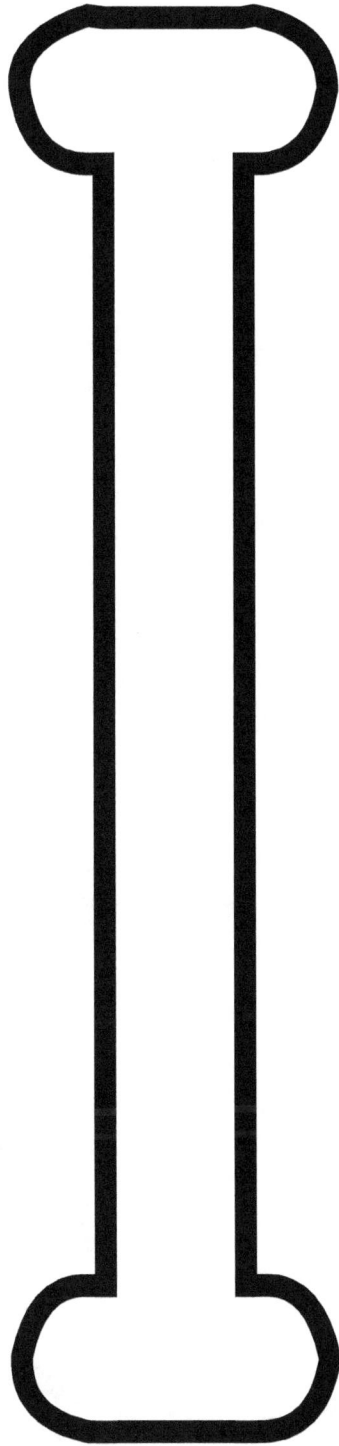

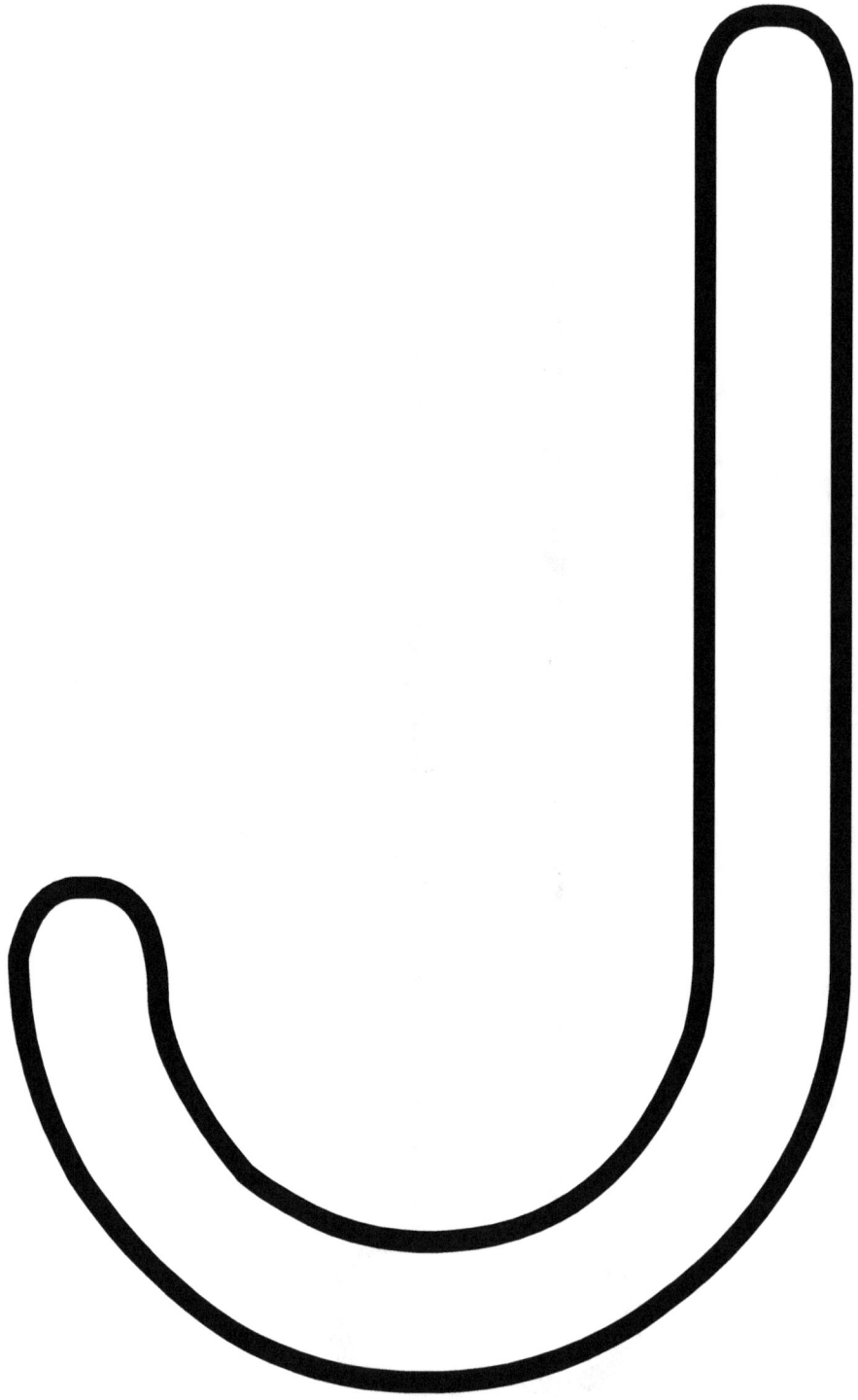

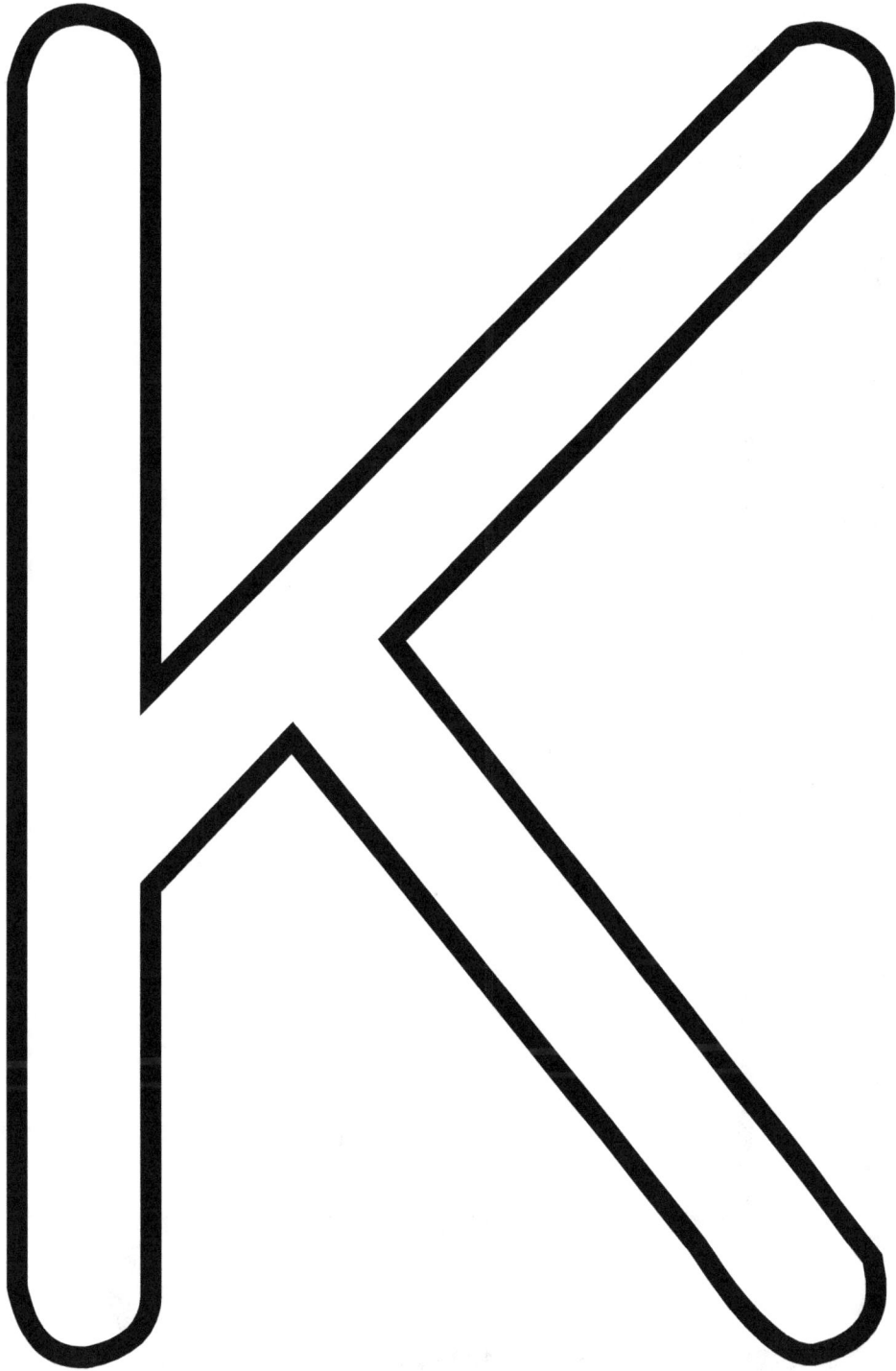

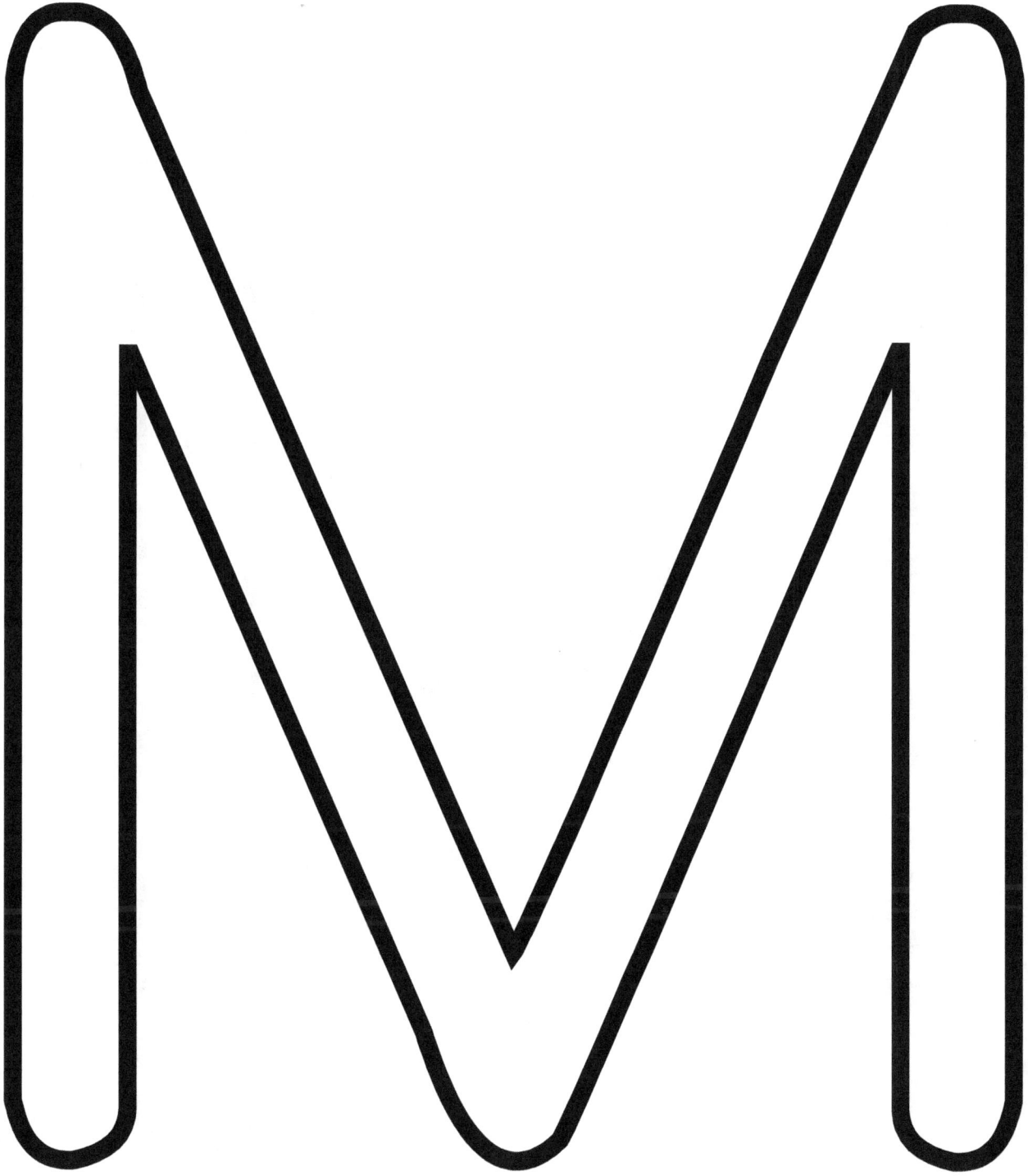

M

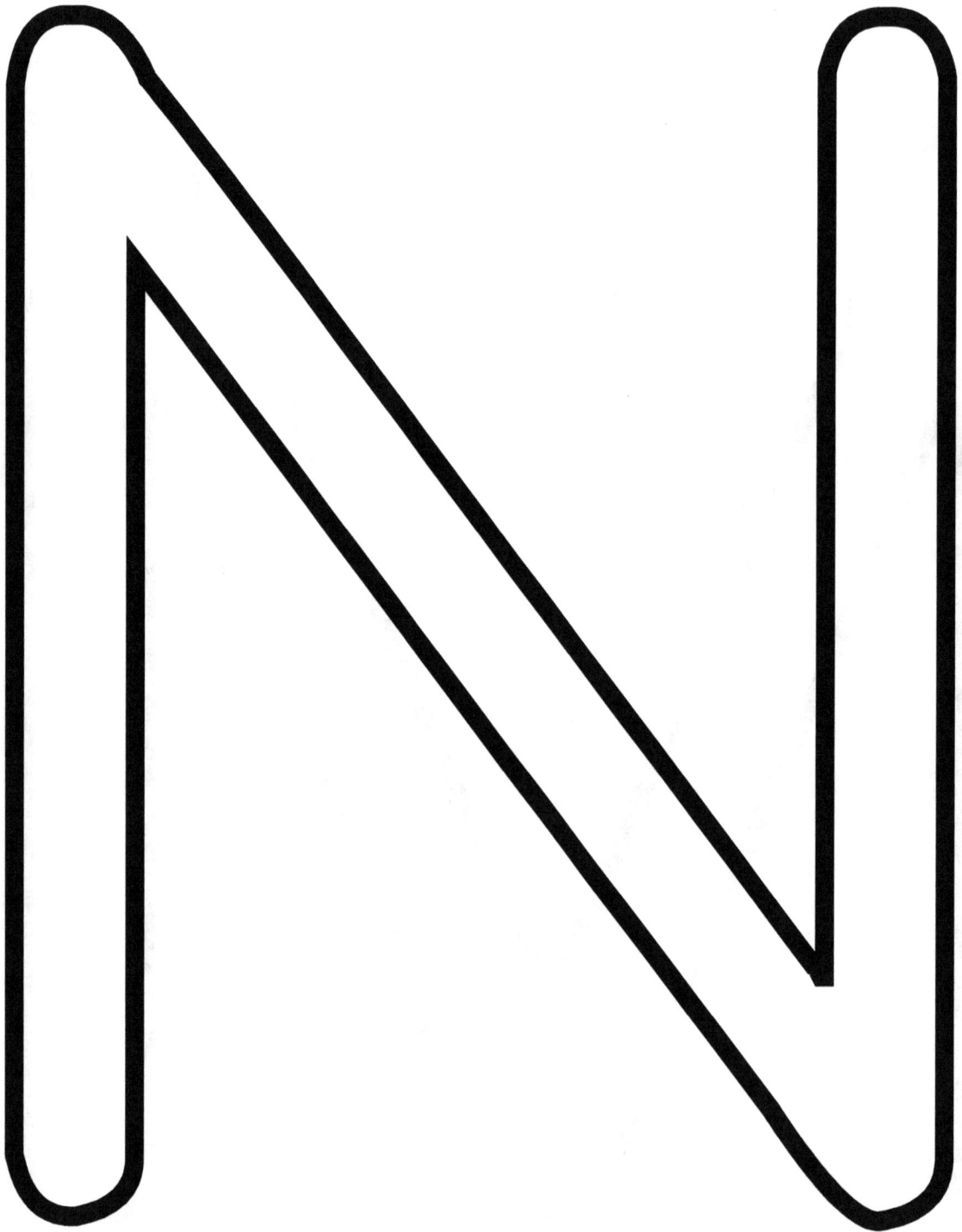

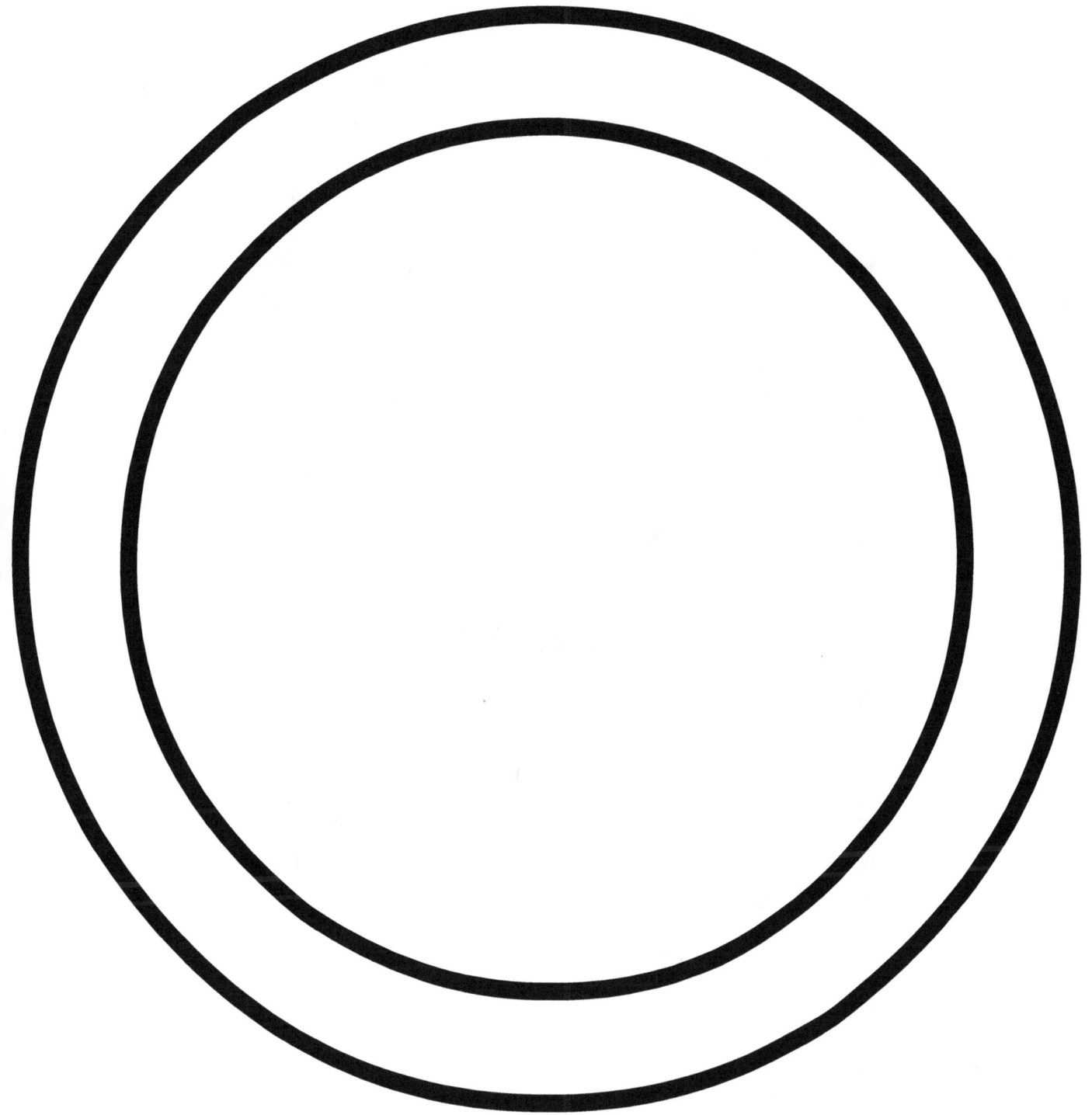

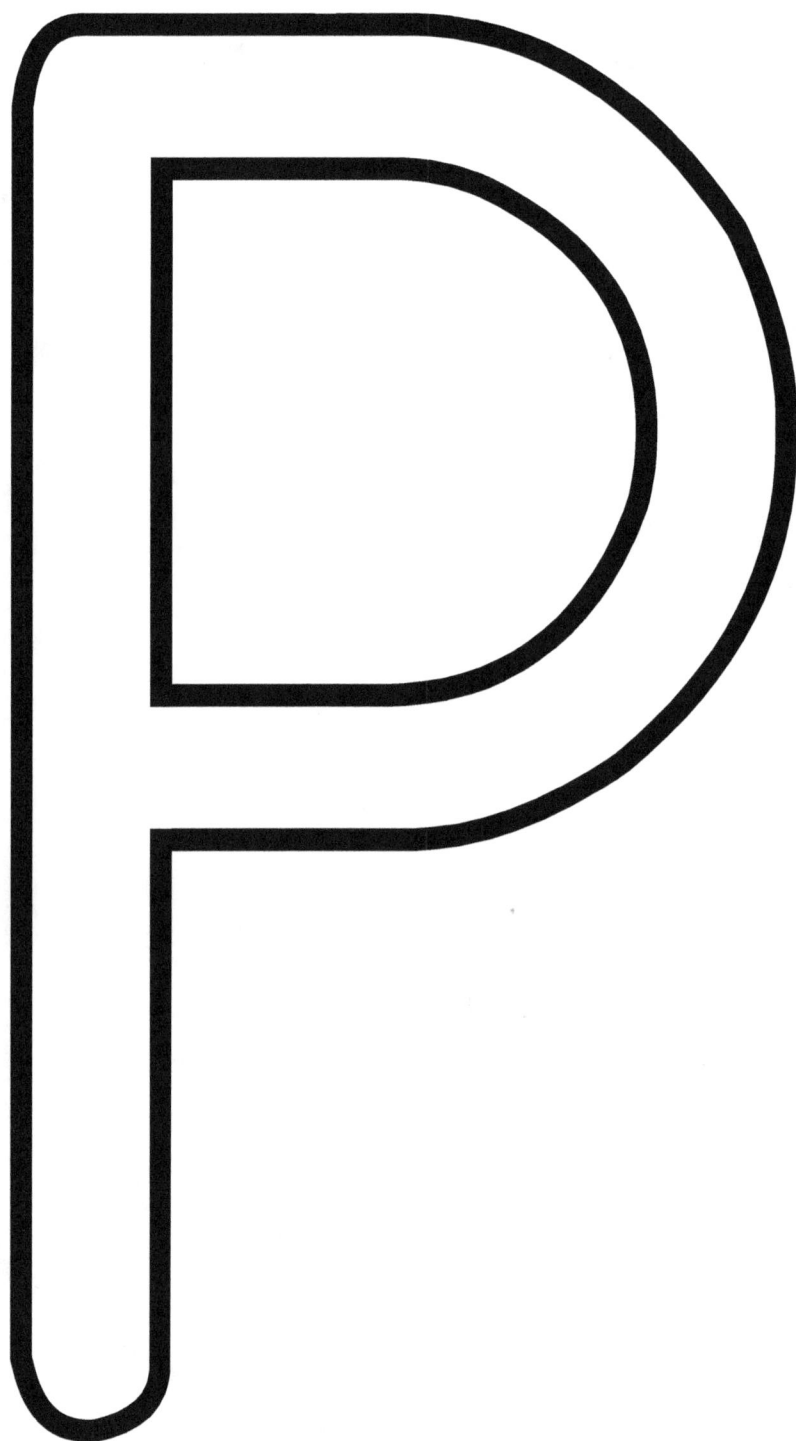

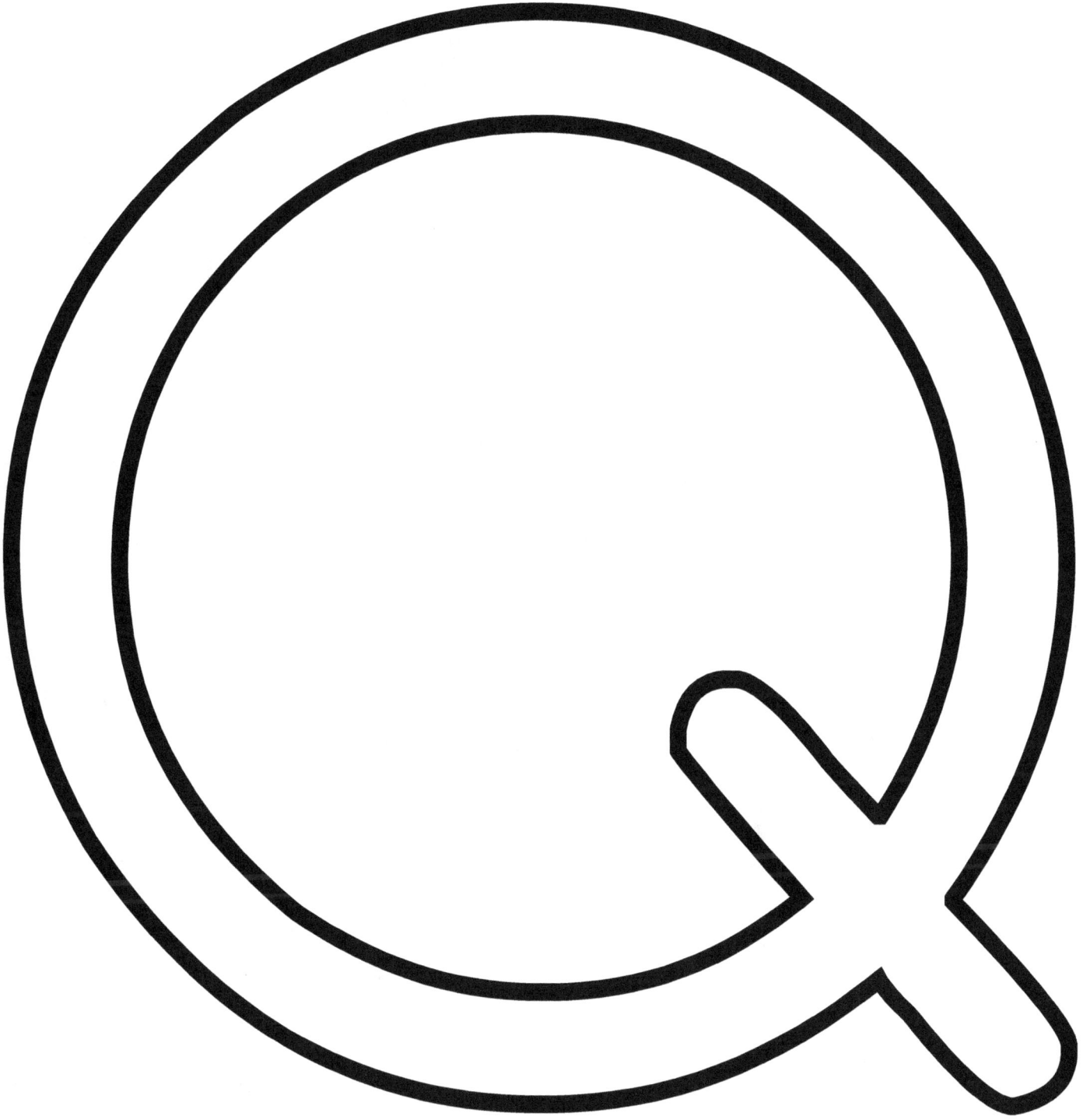

R

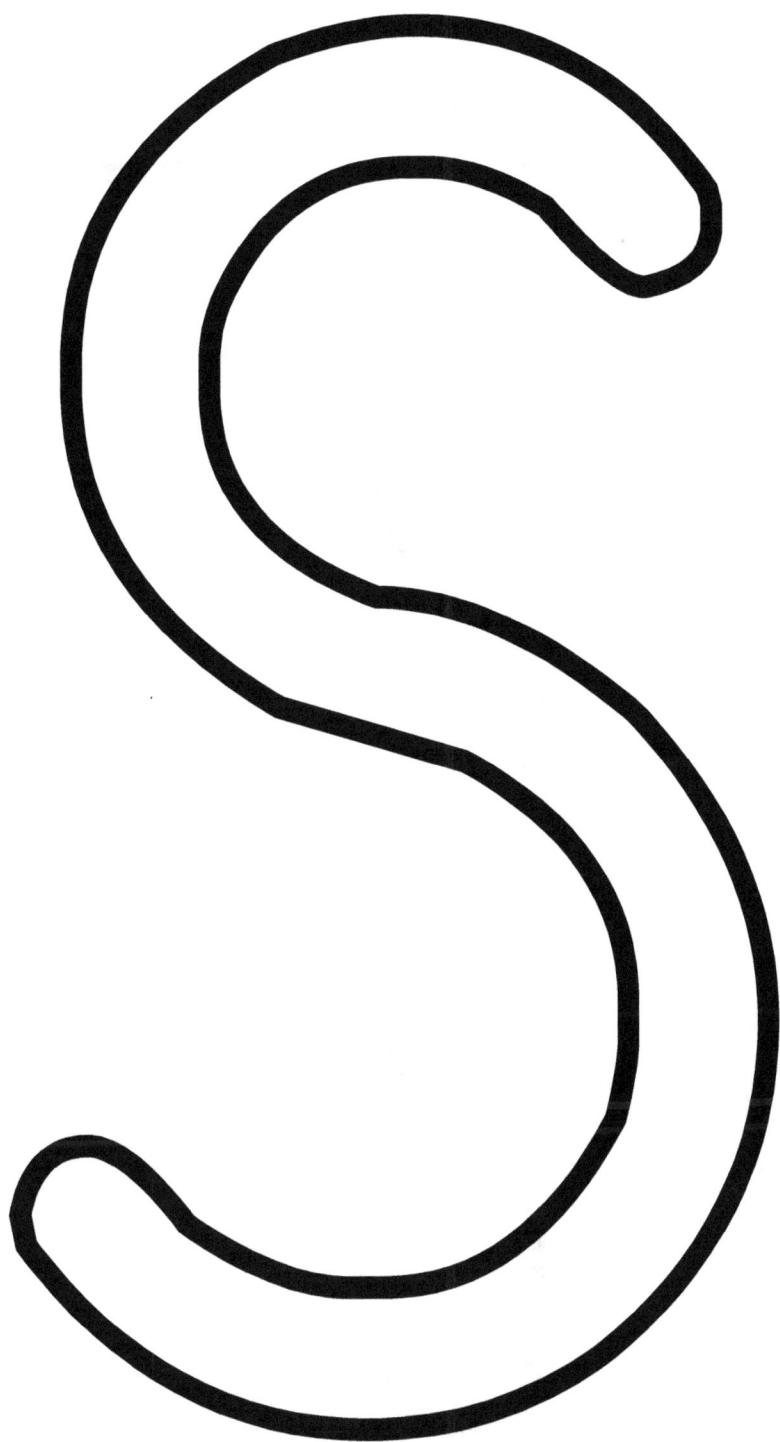

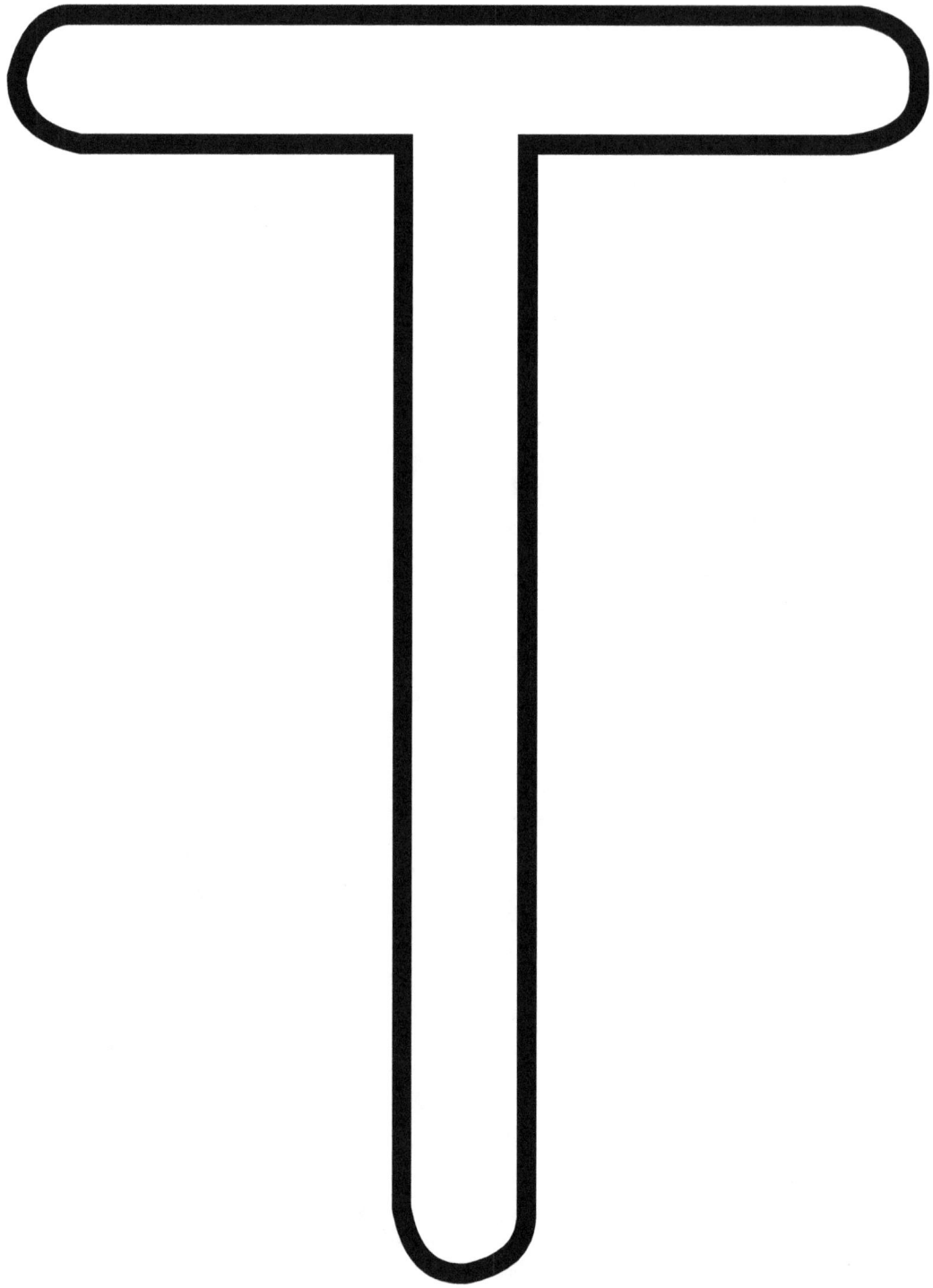

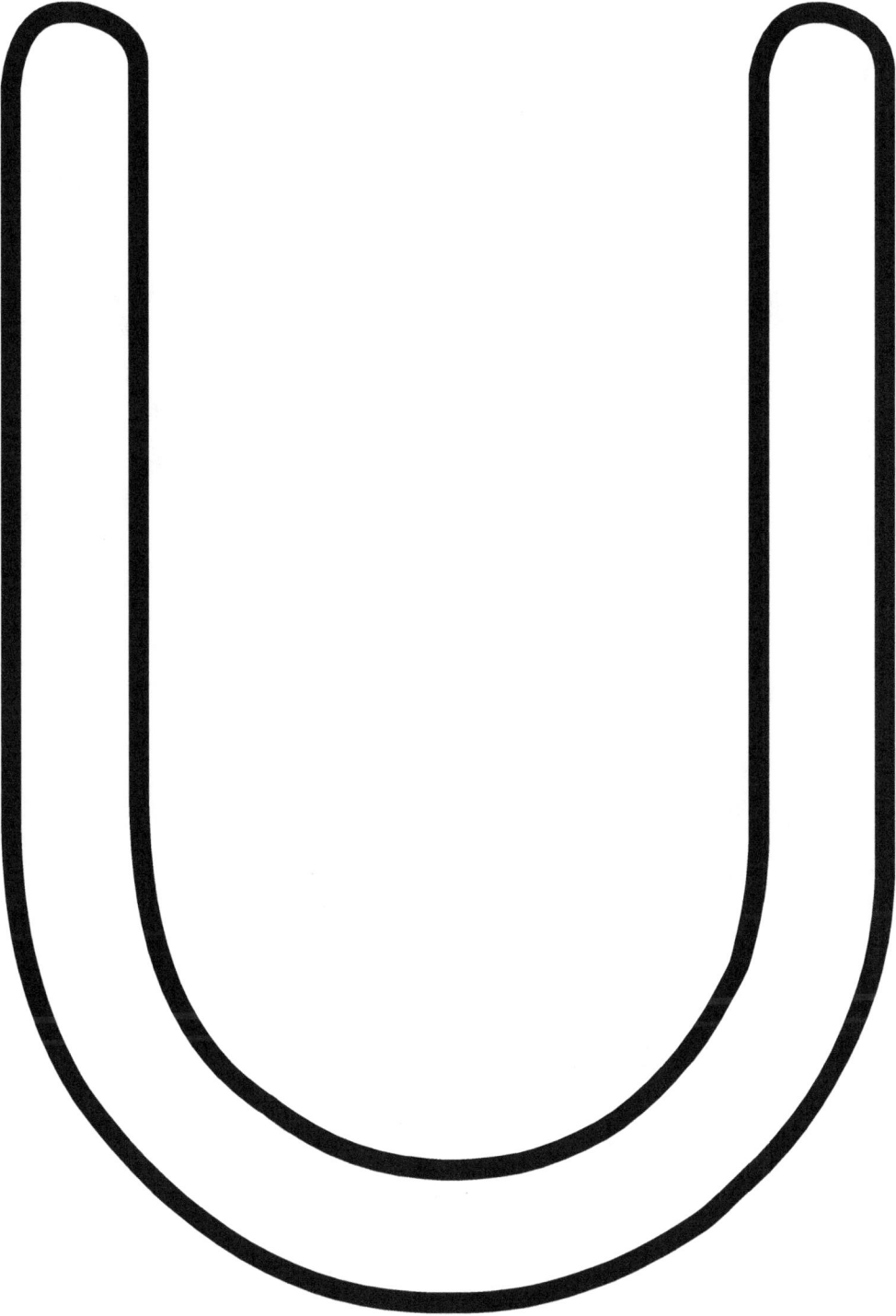

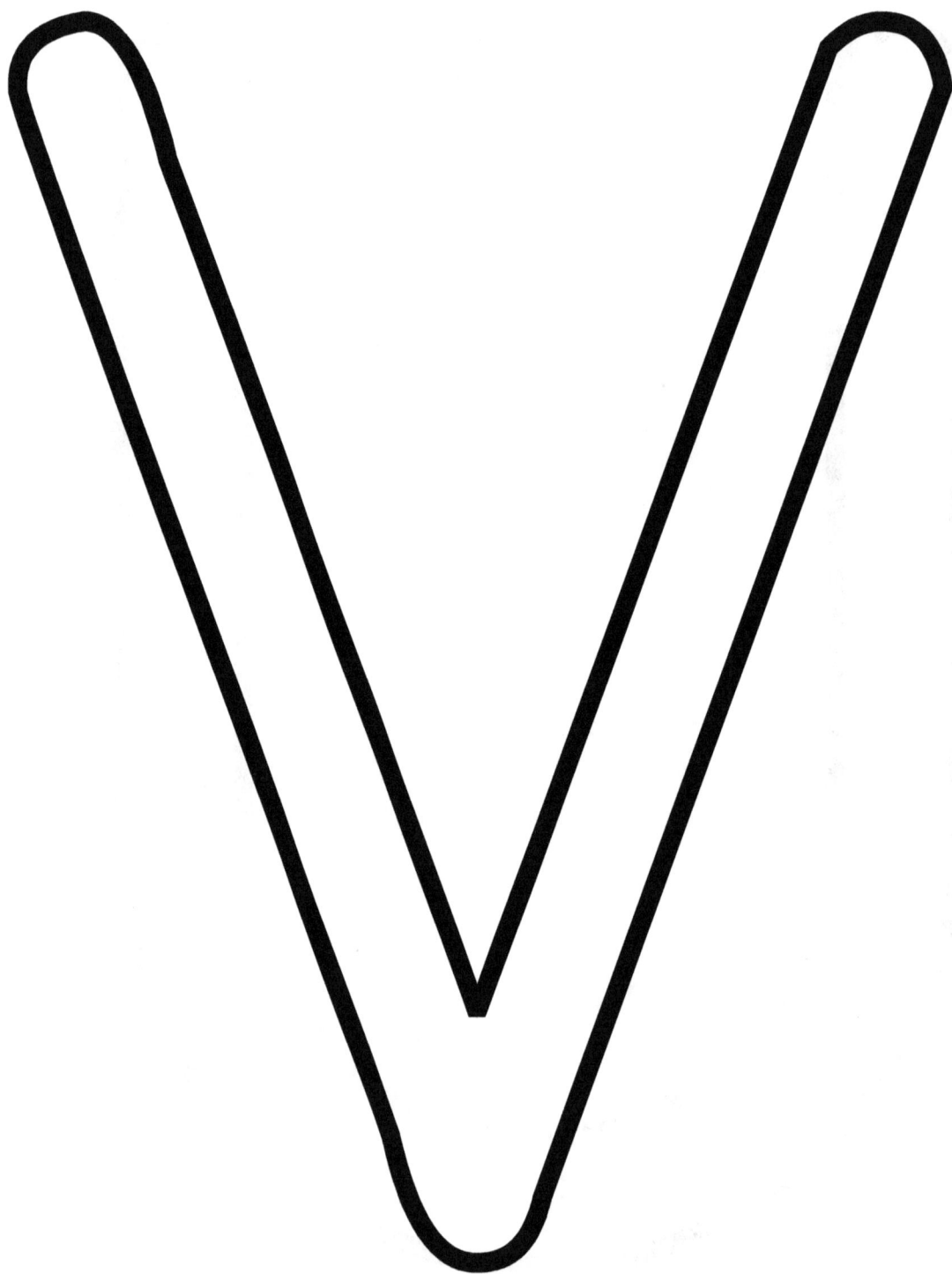

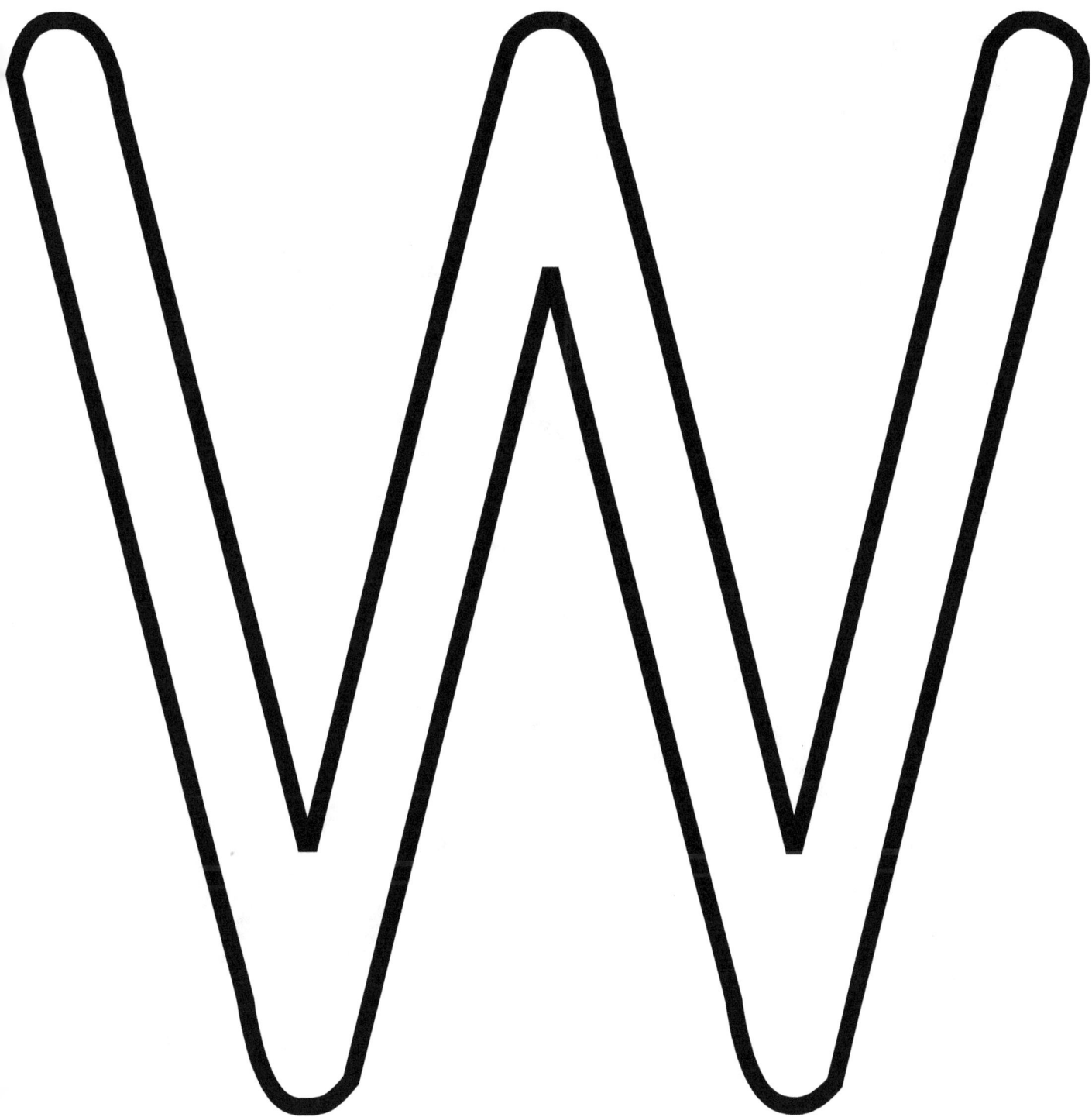

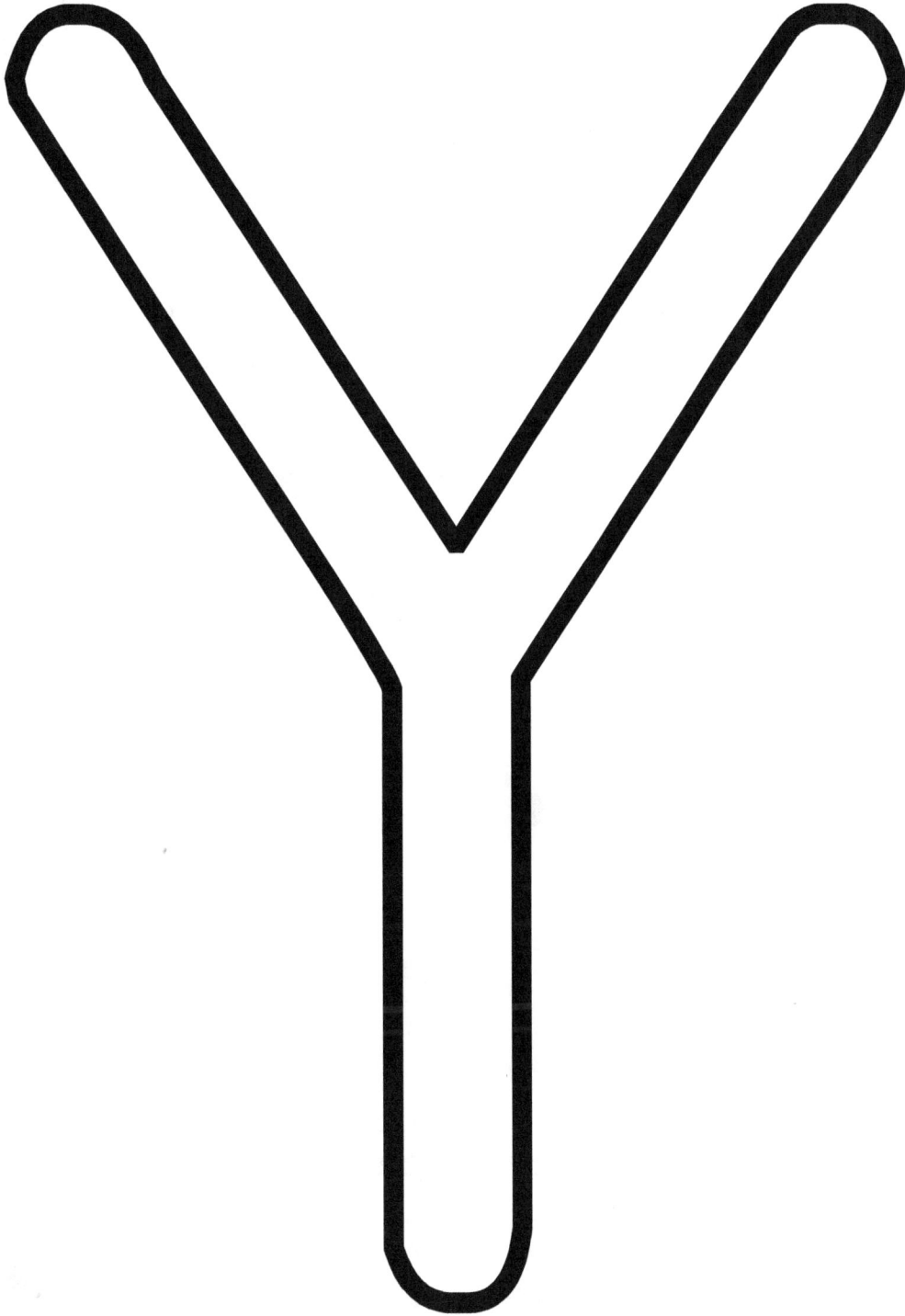

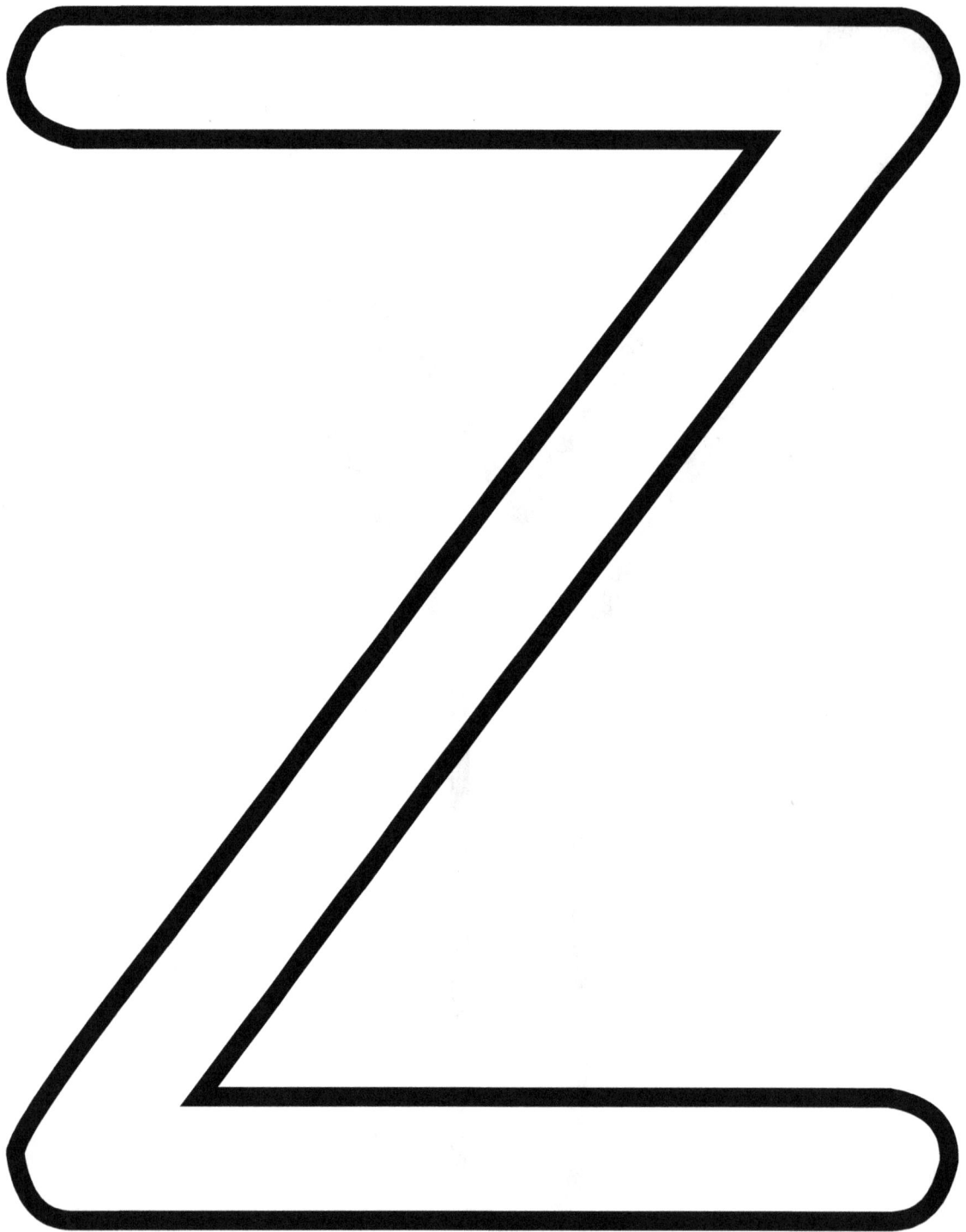

OBJECTS
&
LETTERS

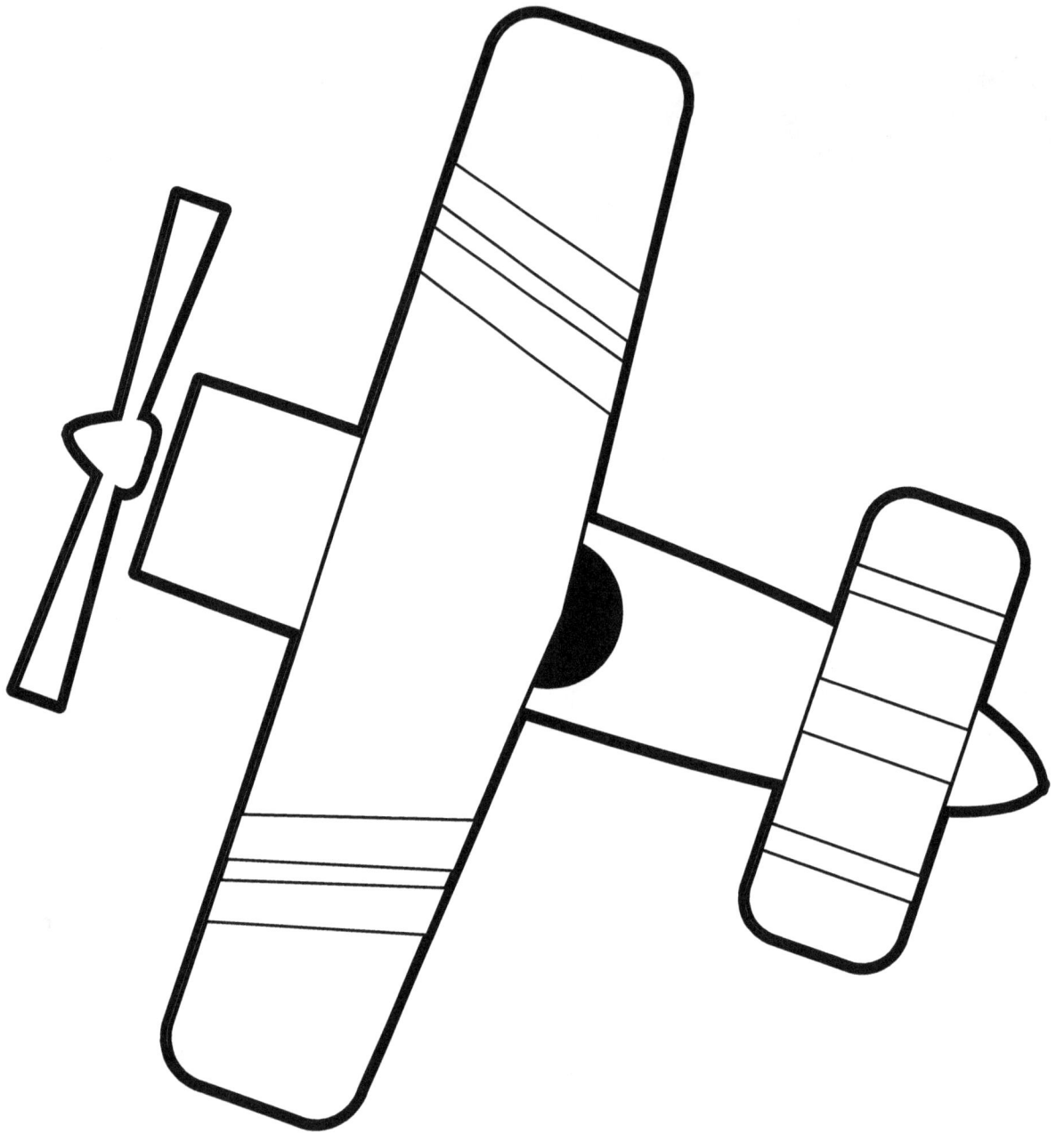

A

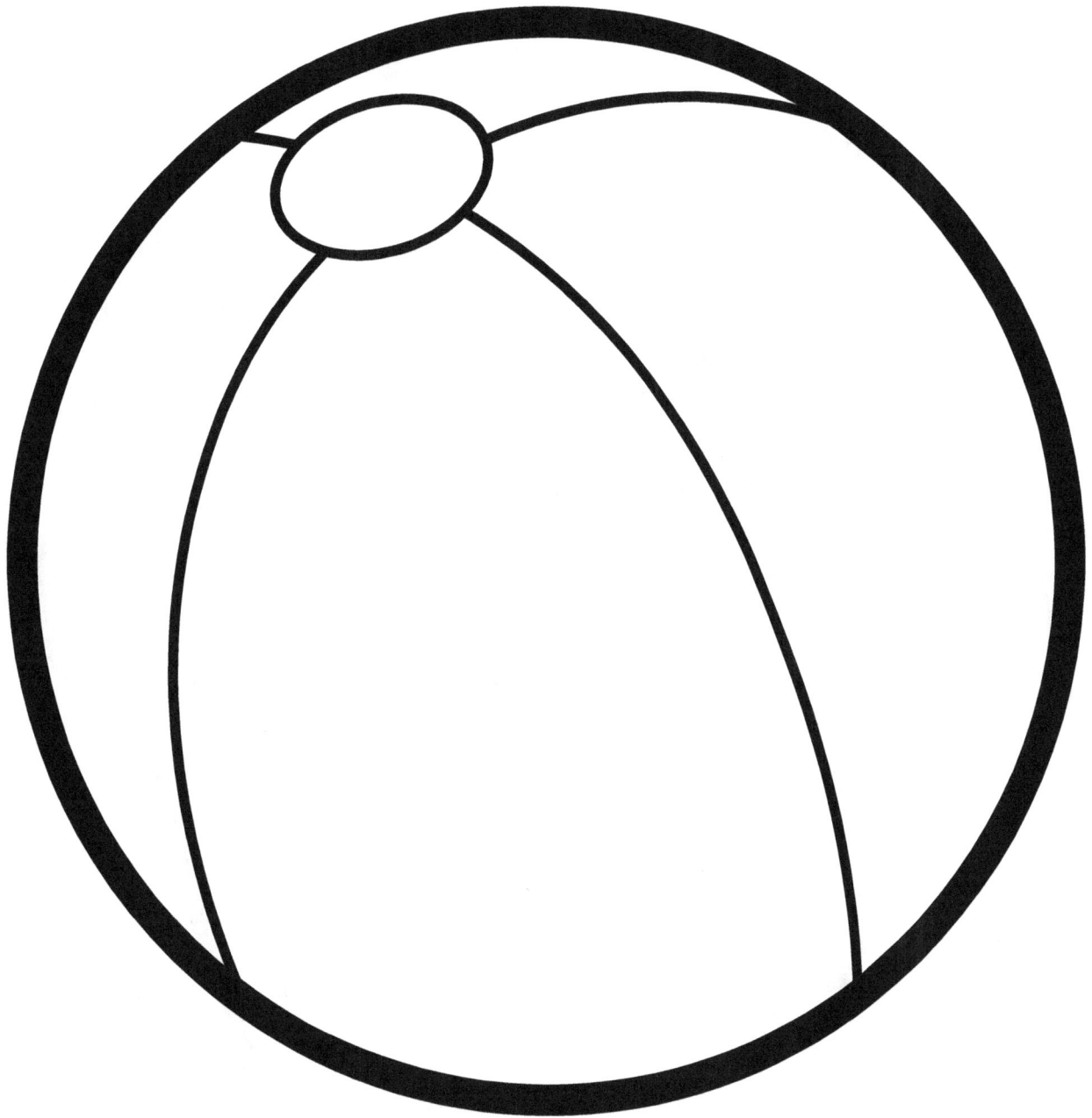

B

C

D

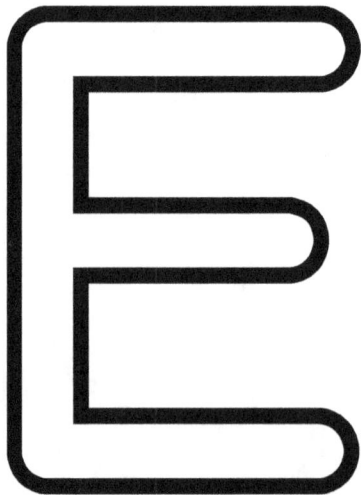

F

G

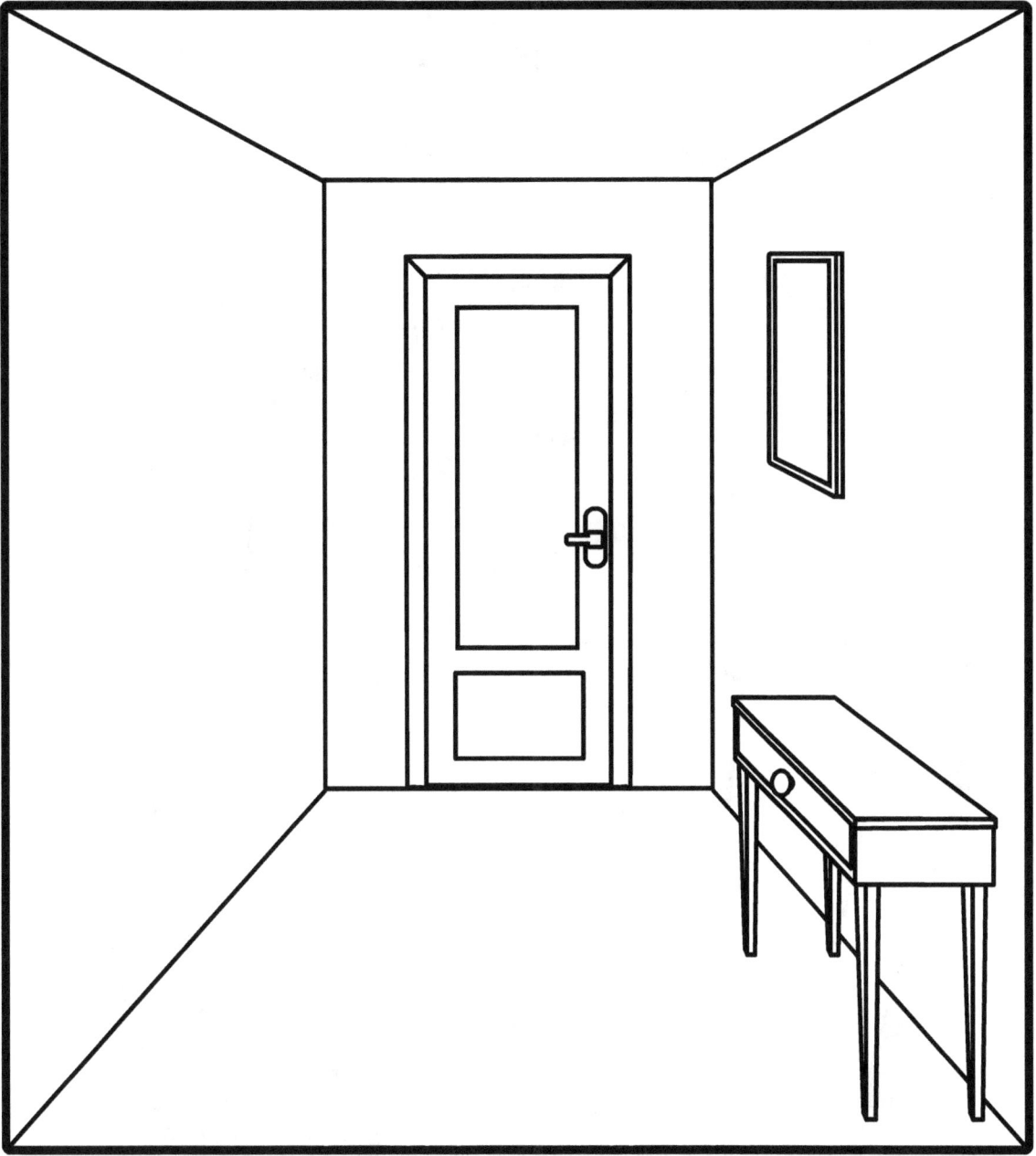

I

J

K

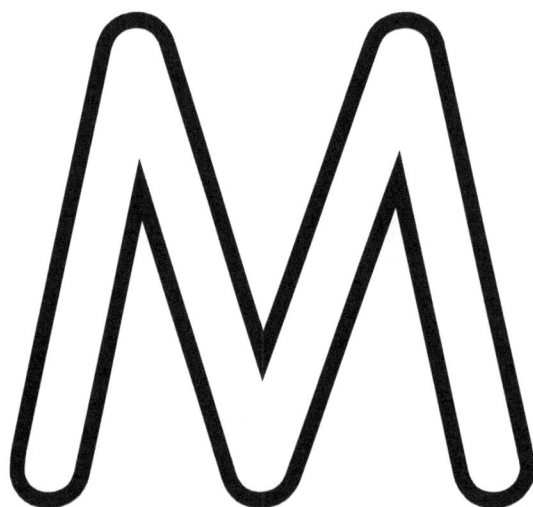

N

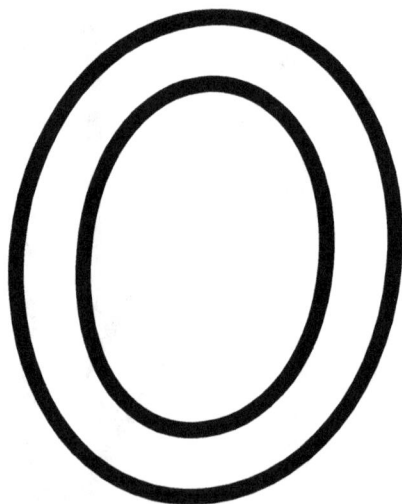

P

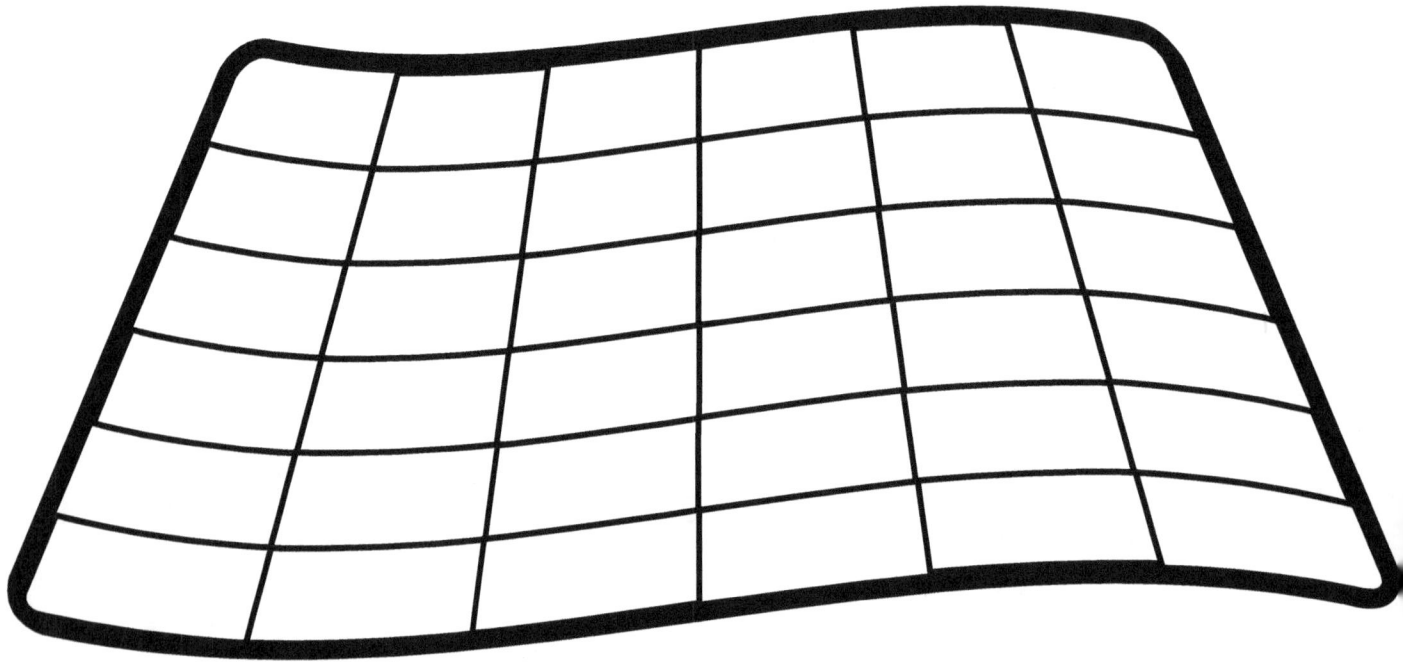

R

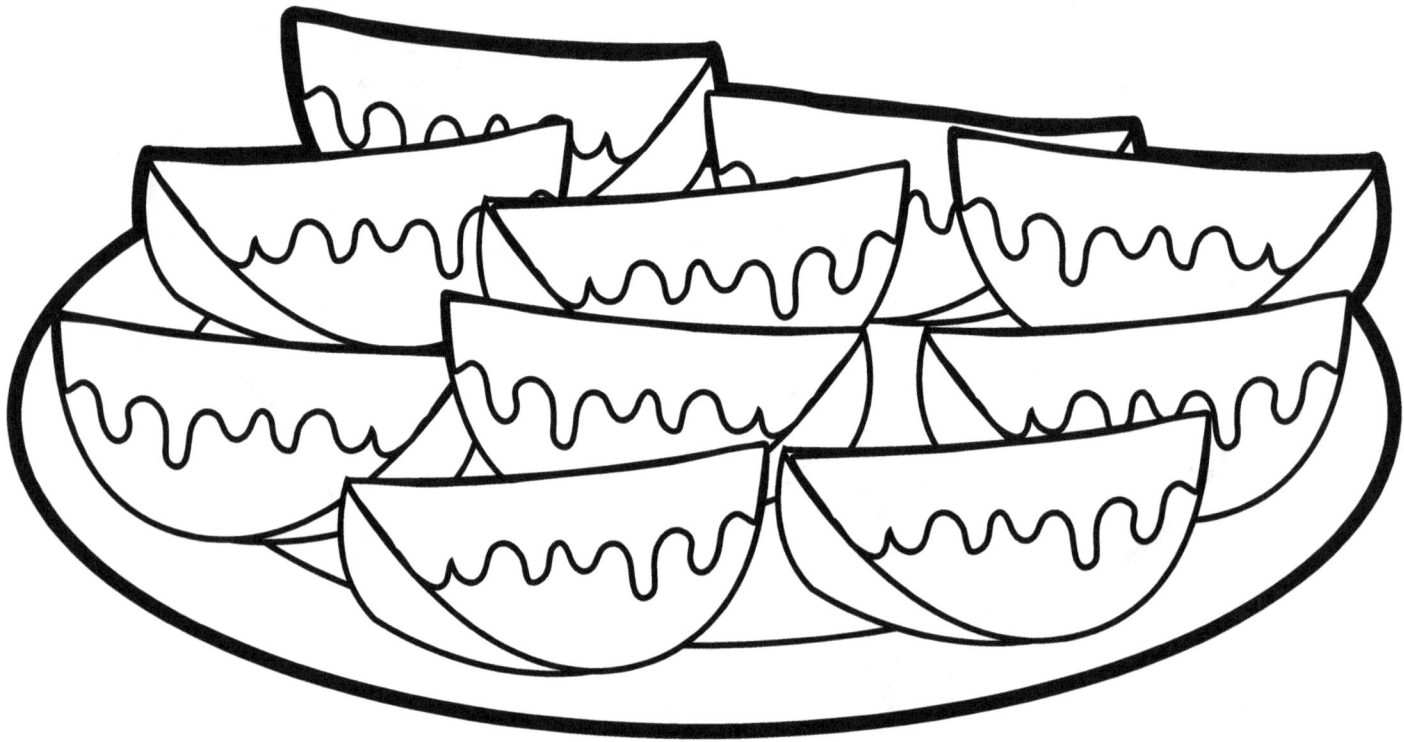

S

T

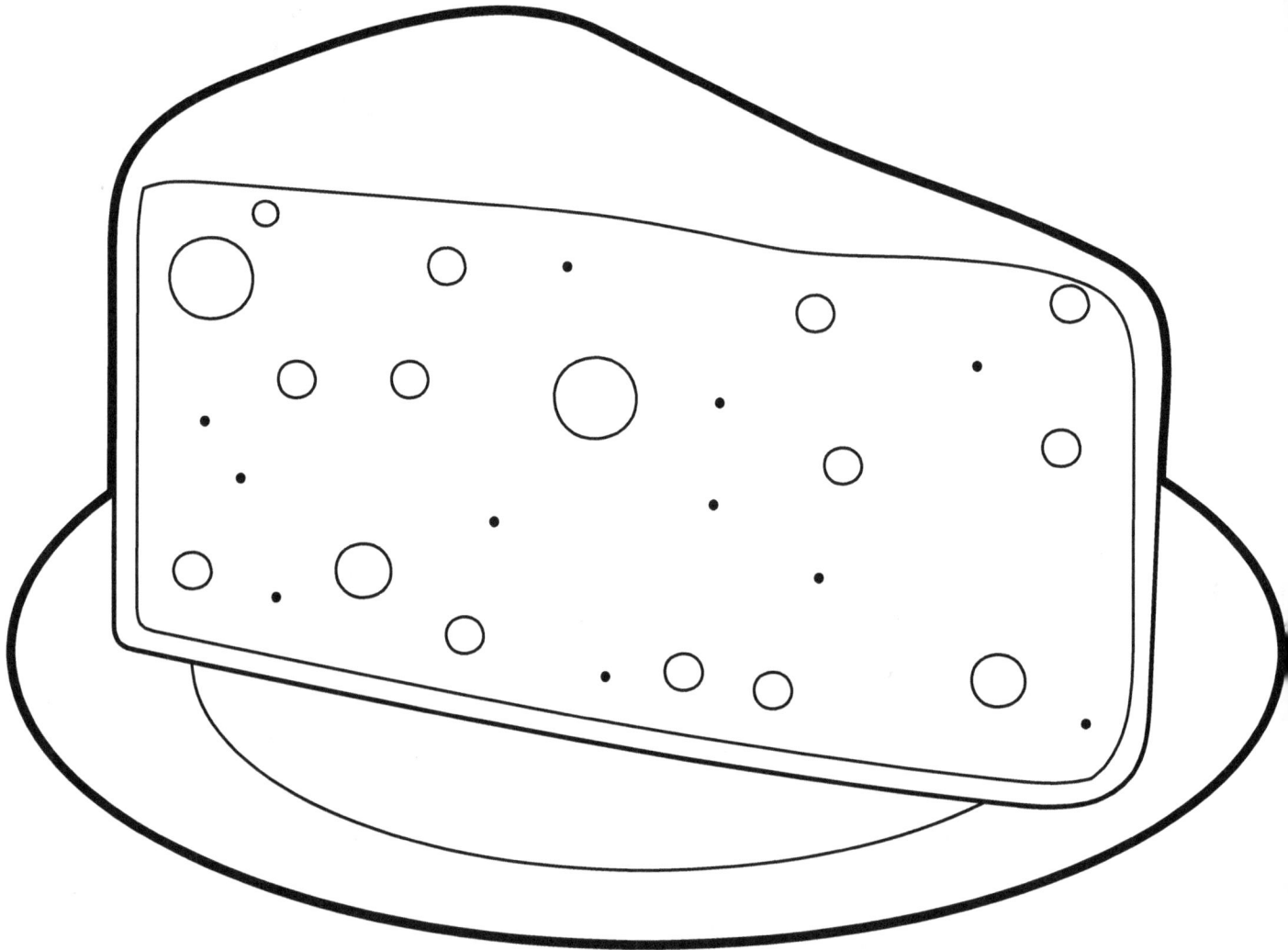

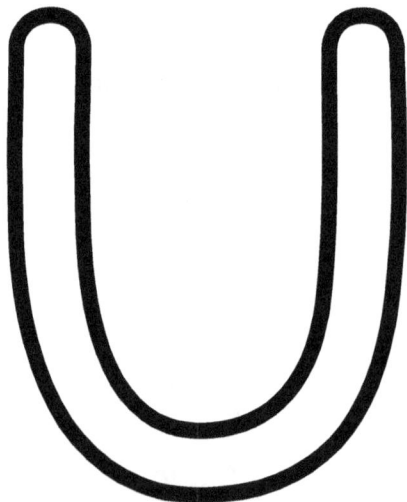

W

Y

Z

SHAPES

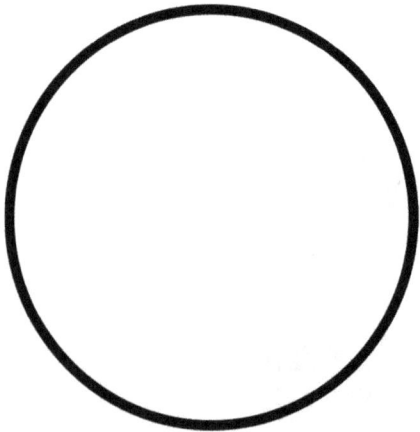

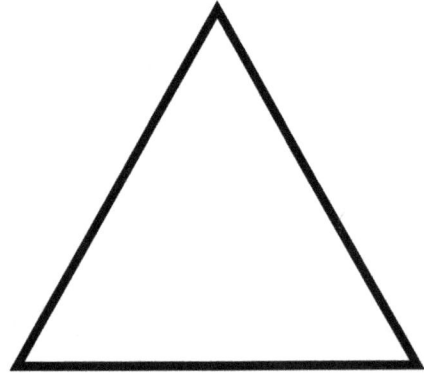

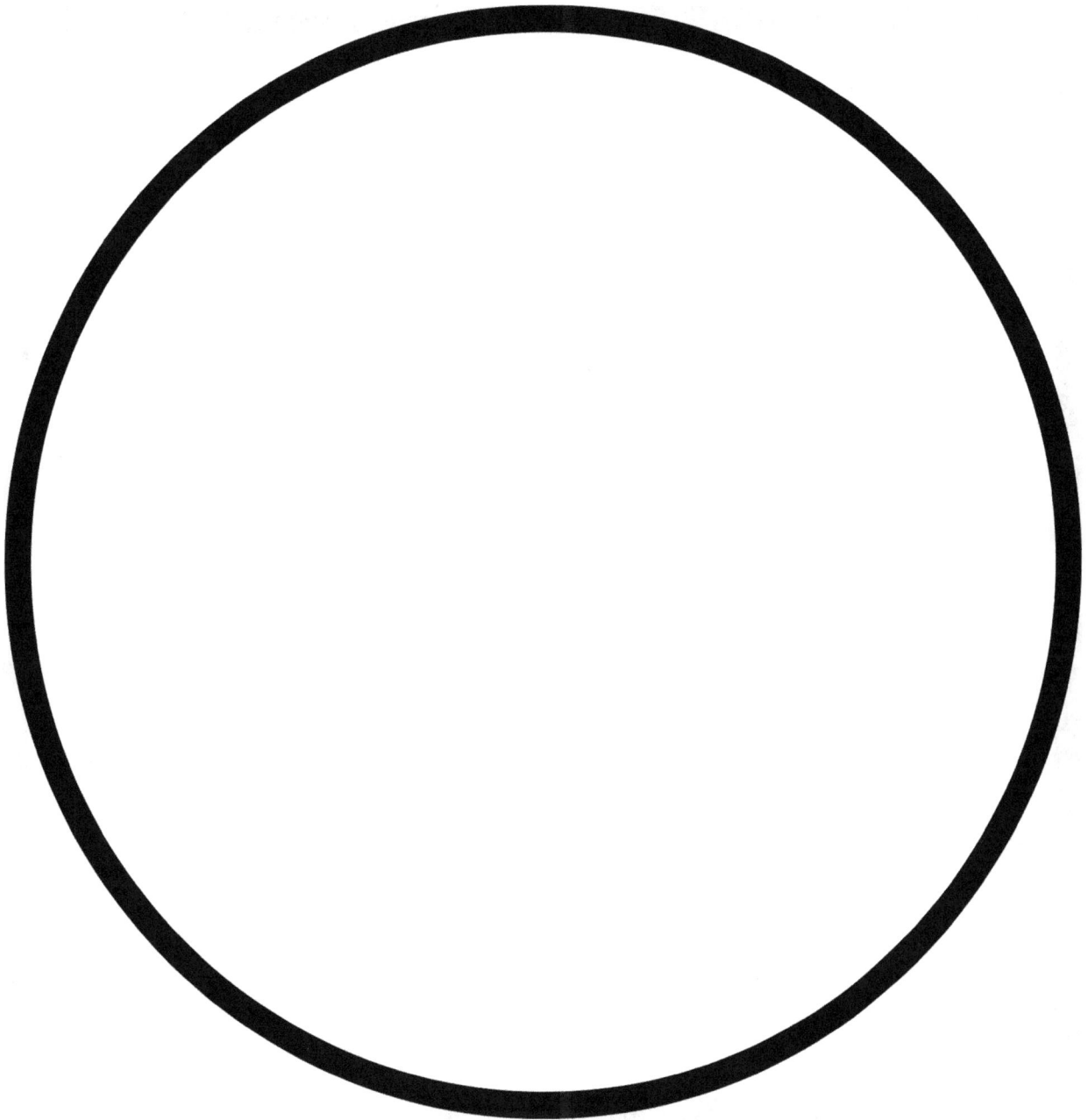

circle

square

rectangle

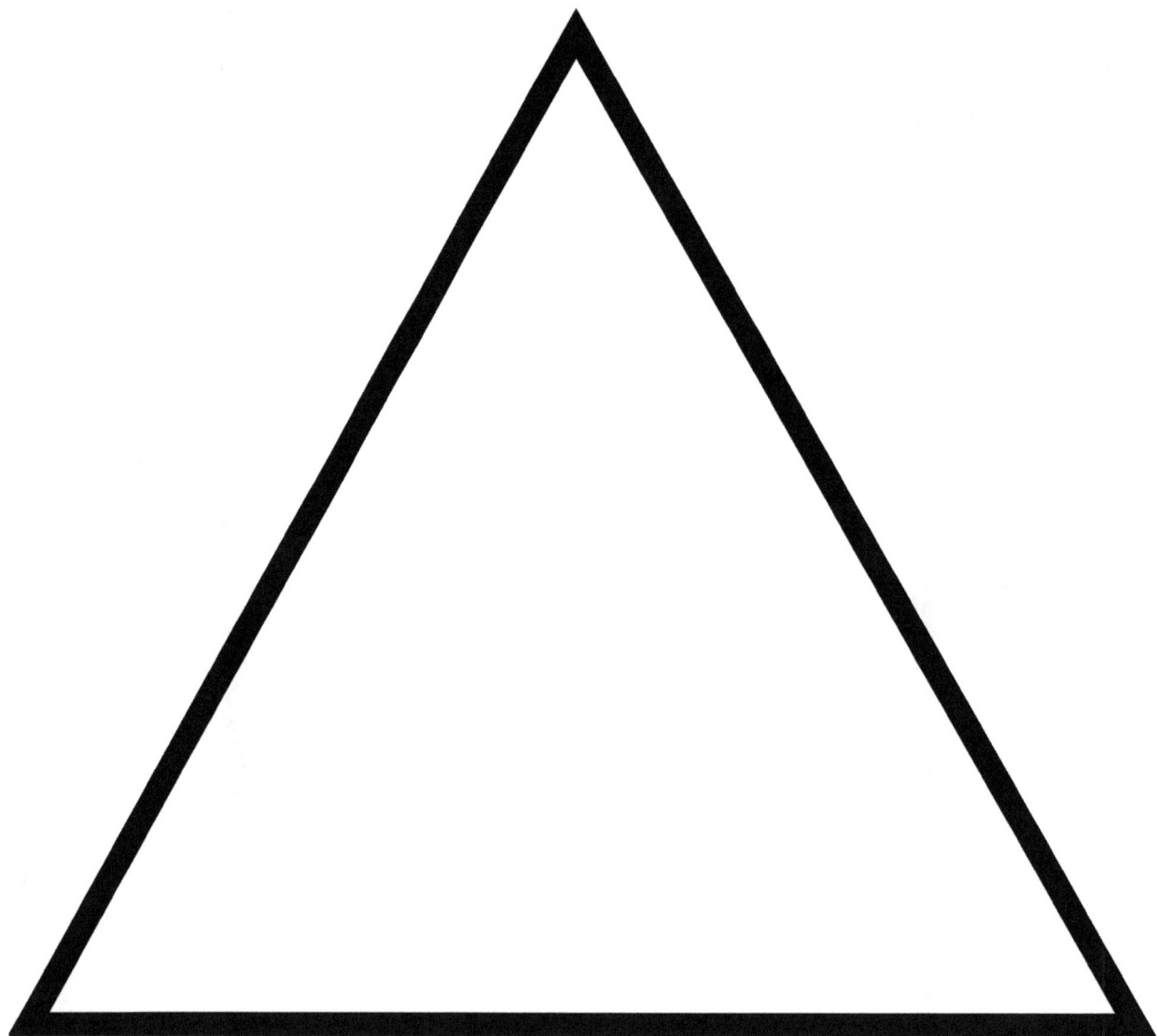

triangle

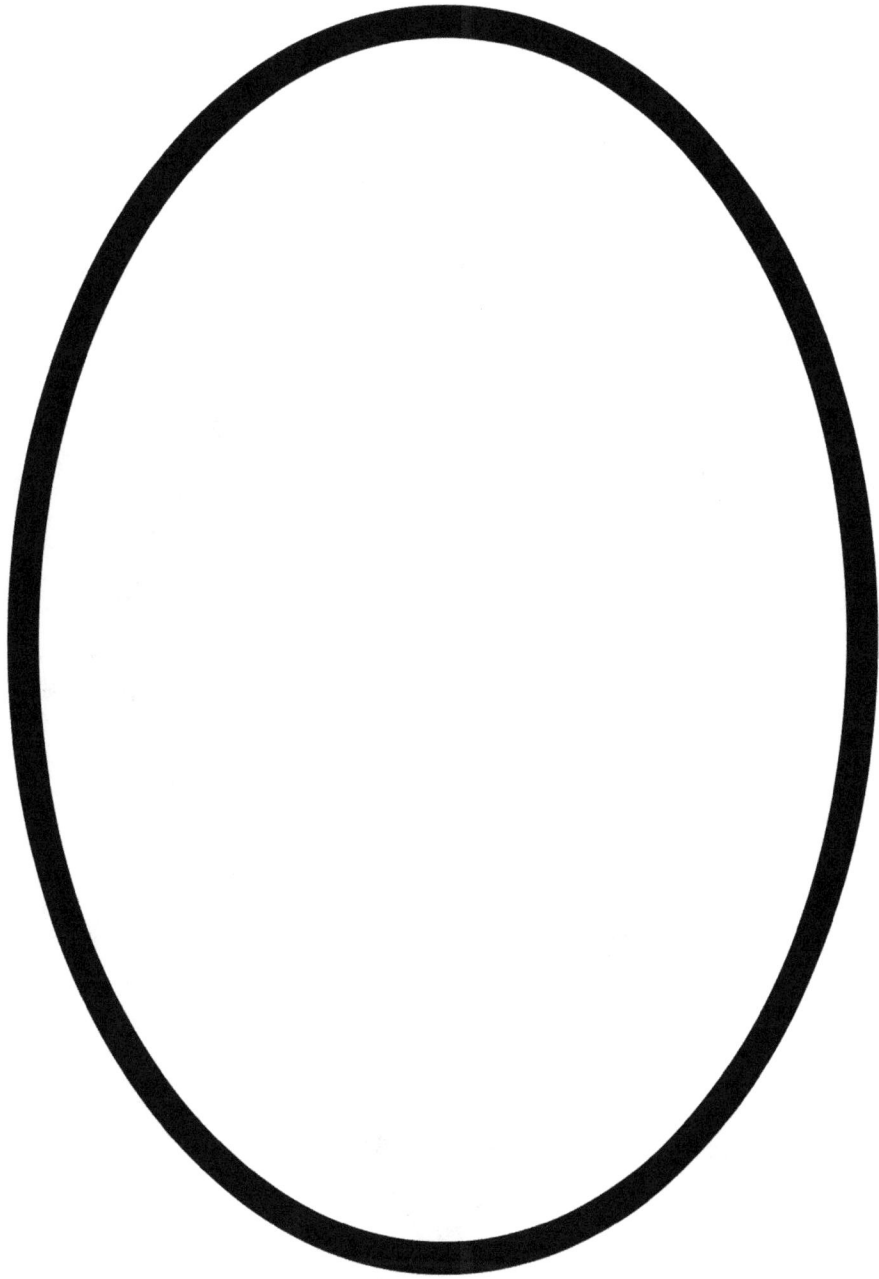

oval

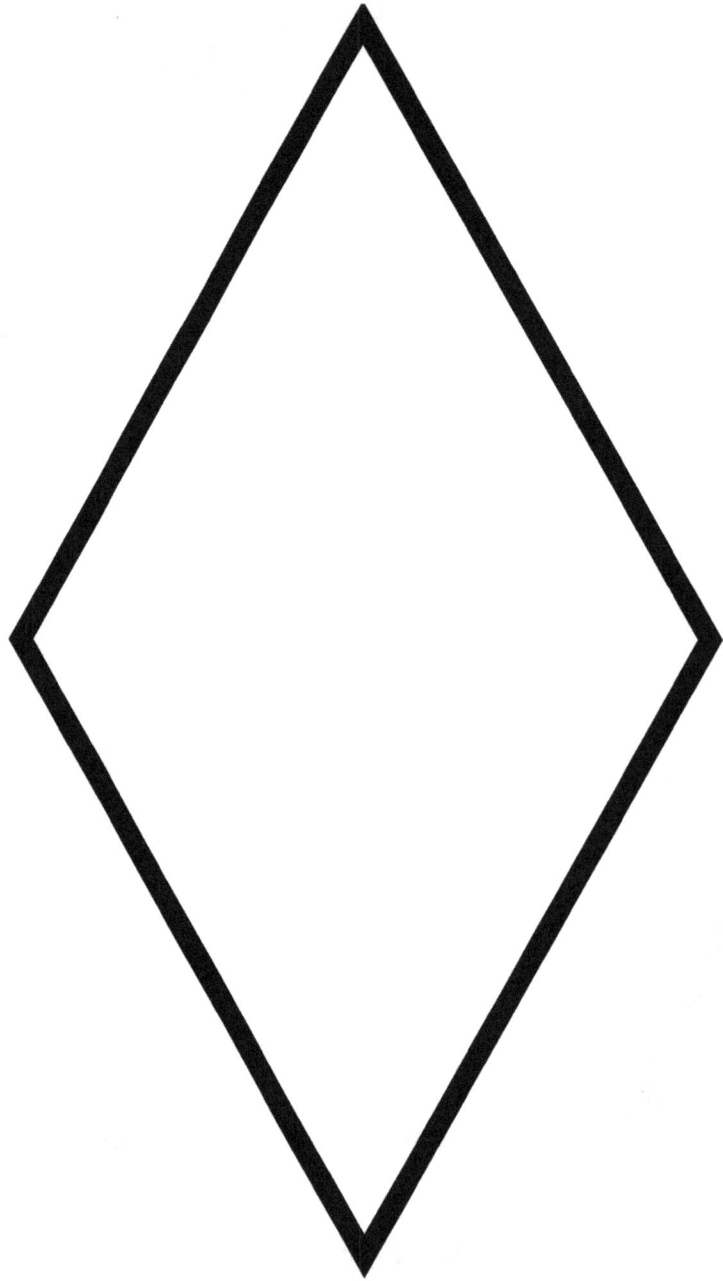

diamond

heart

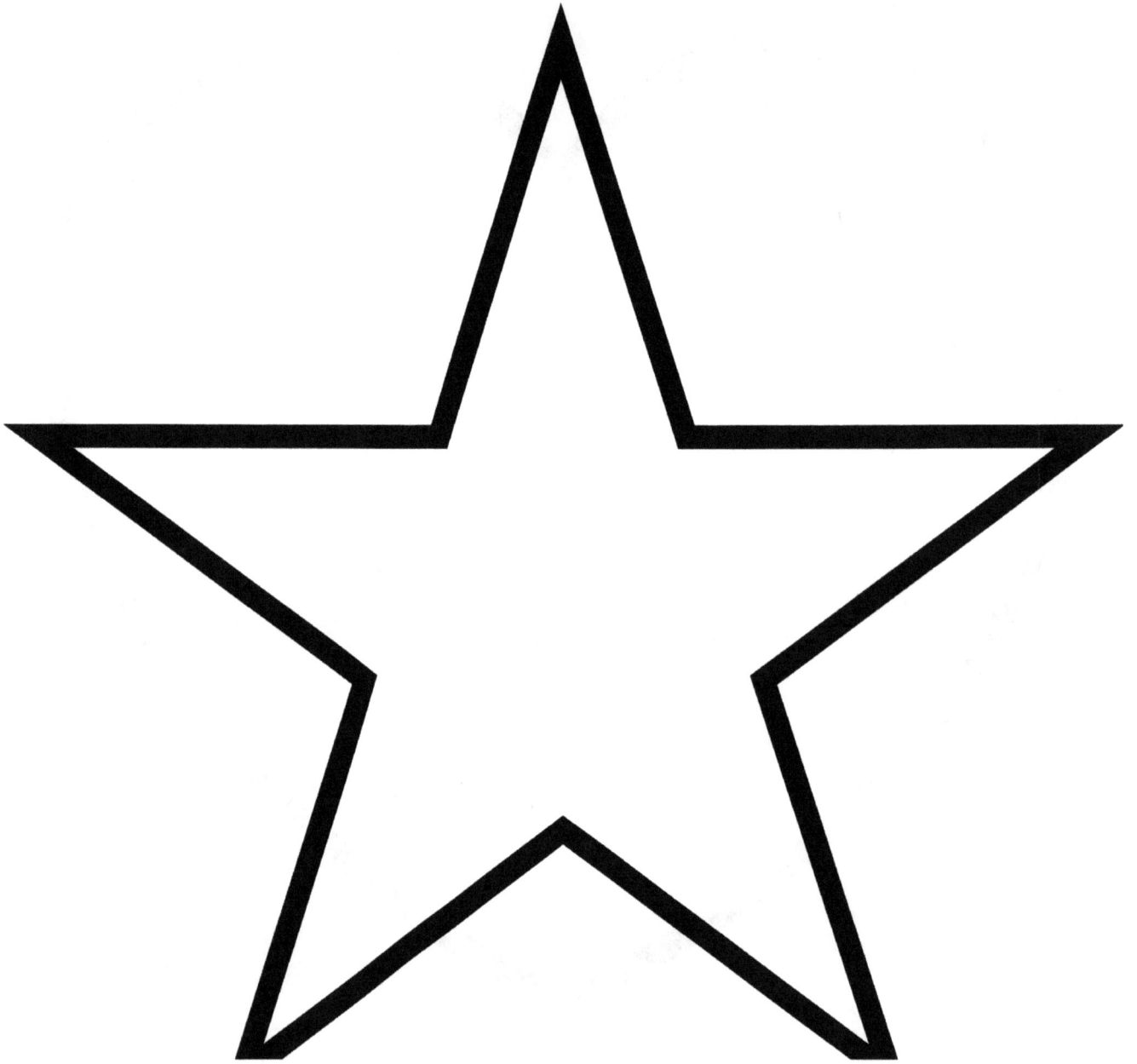

star

COUNTING SHAPES

1   3

2

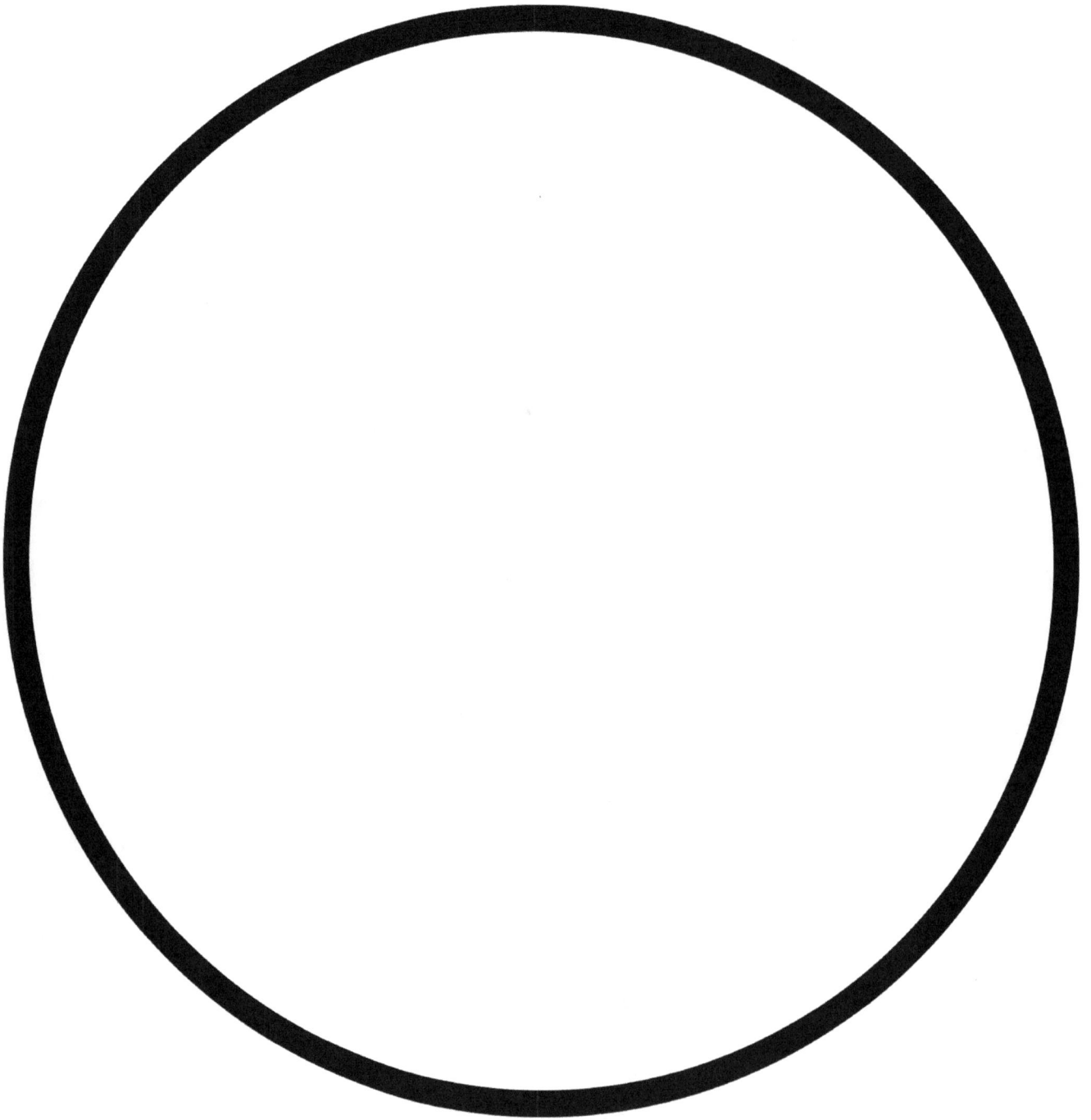

1 circle

2 squares

3 rectangles

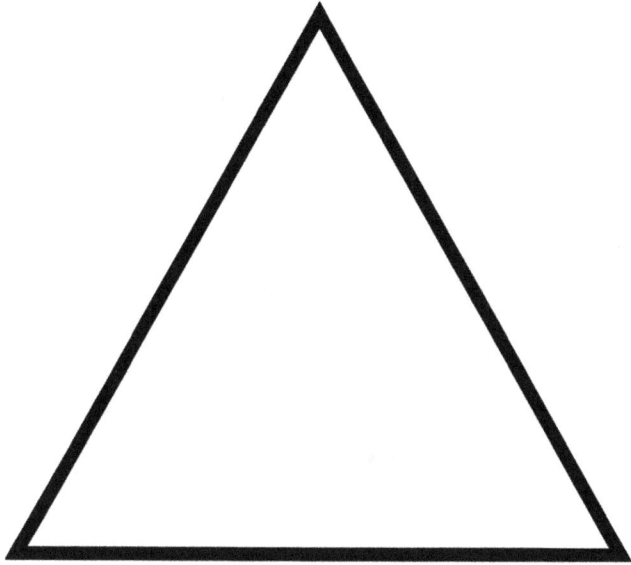

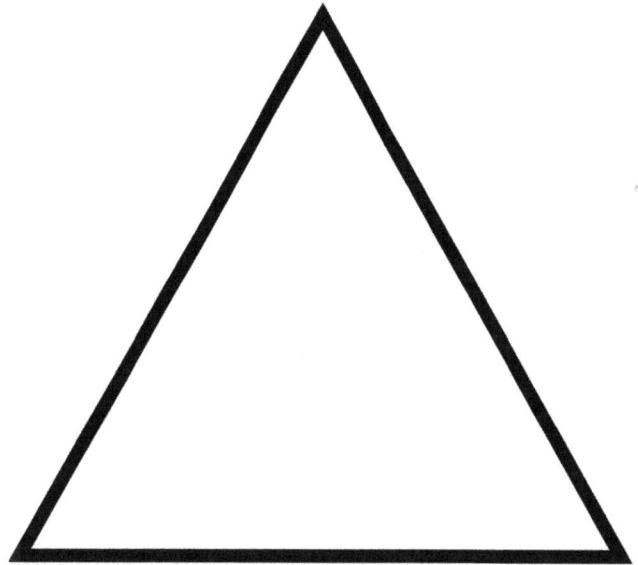

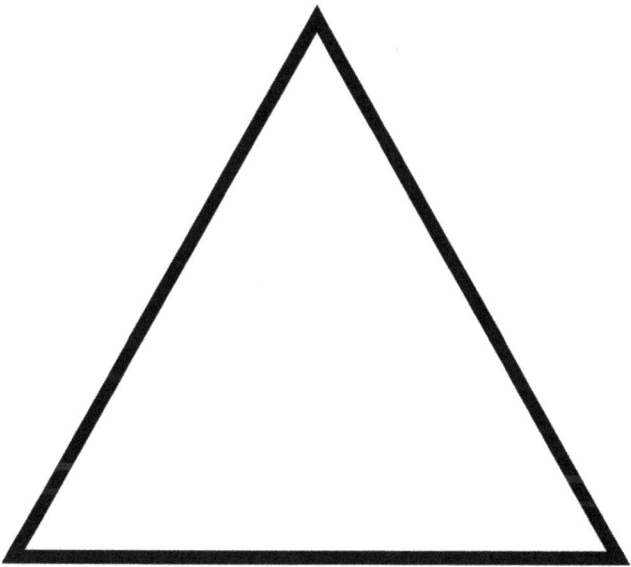

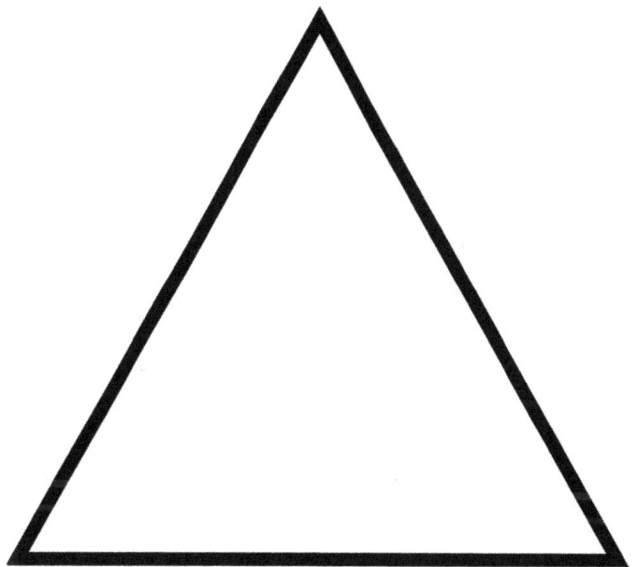

4 triangles

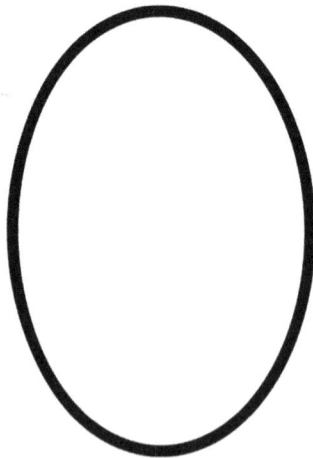

5 ovals

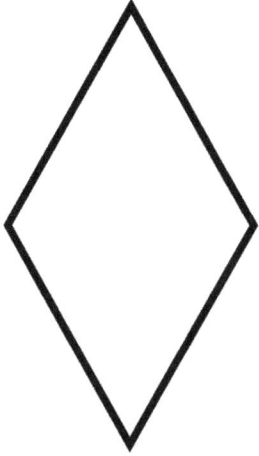

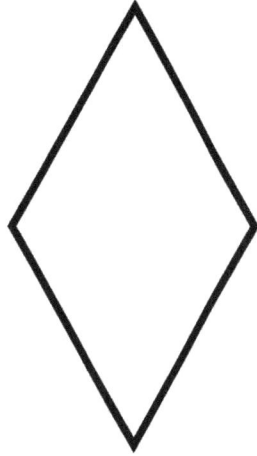

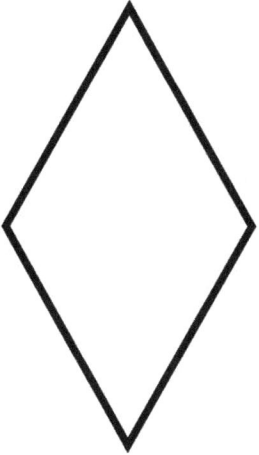

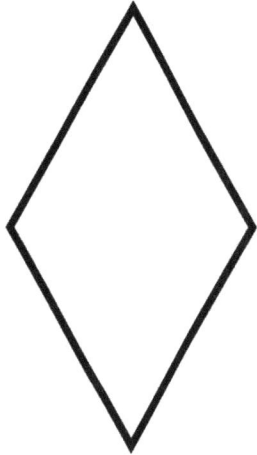

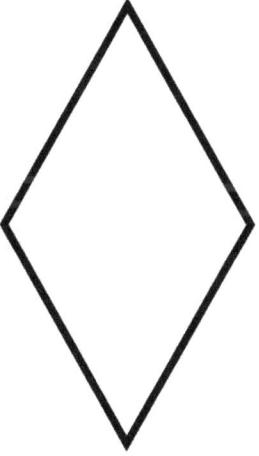

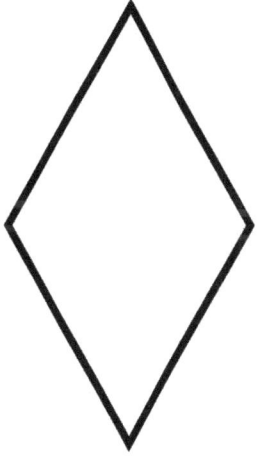

6 diamonds

7 hearts

8 stars

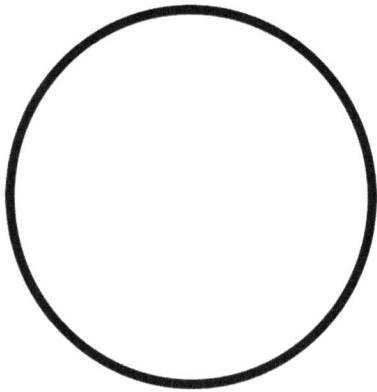

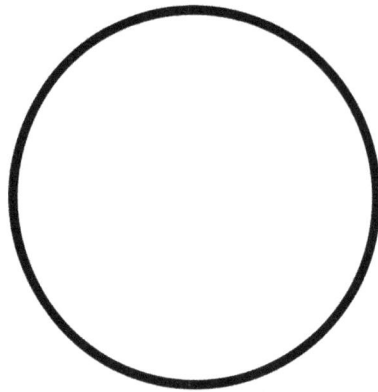

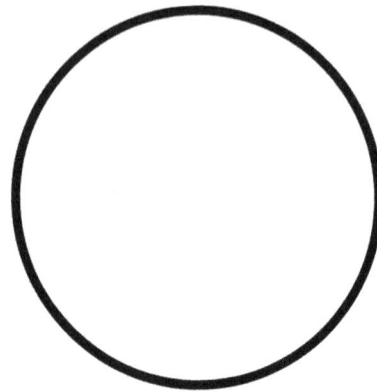

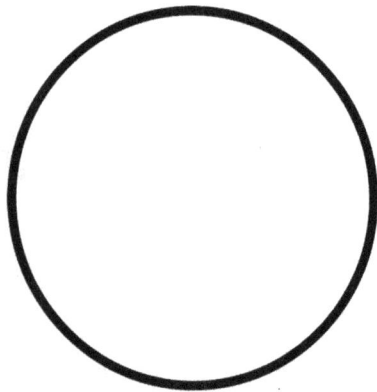

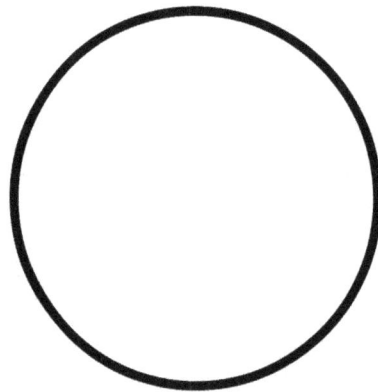

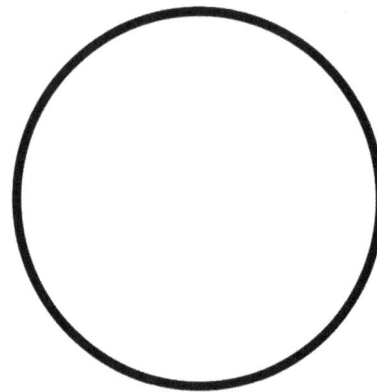

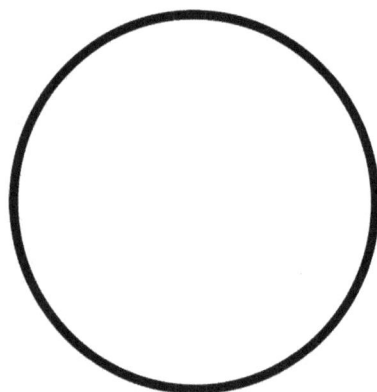

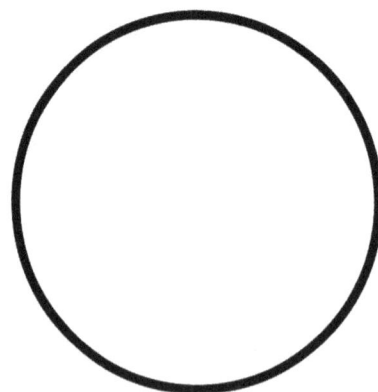

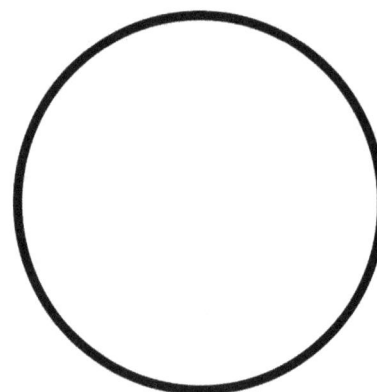

9 circles

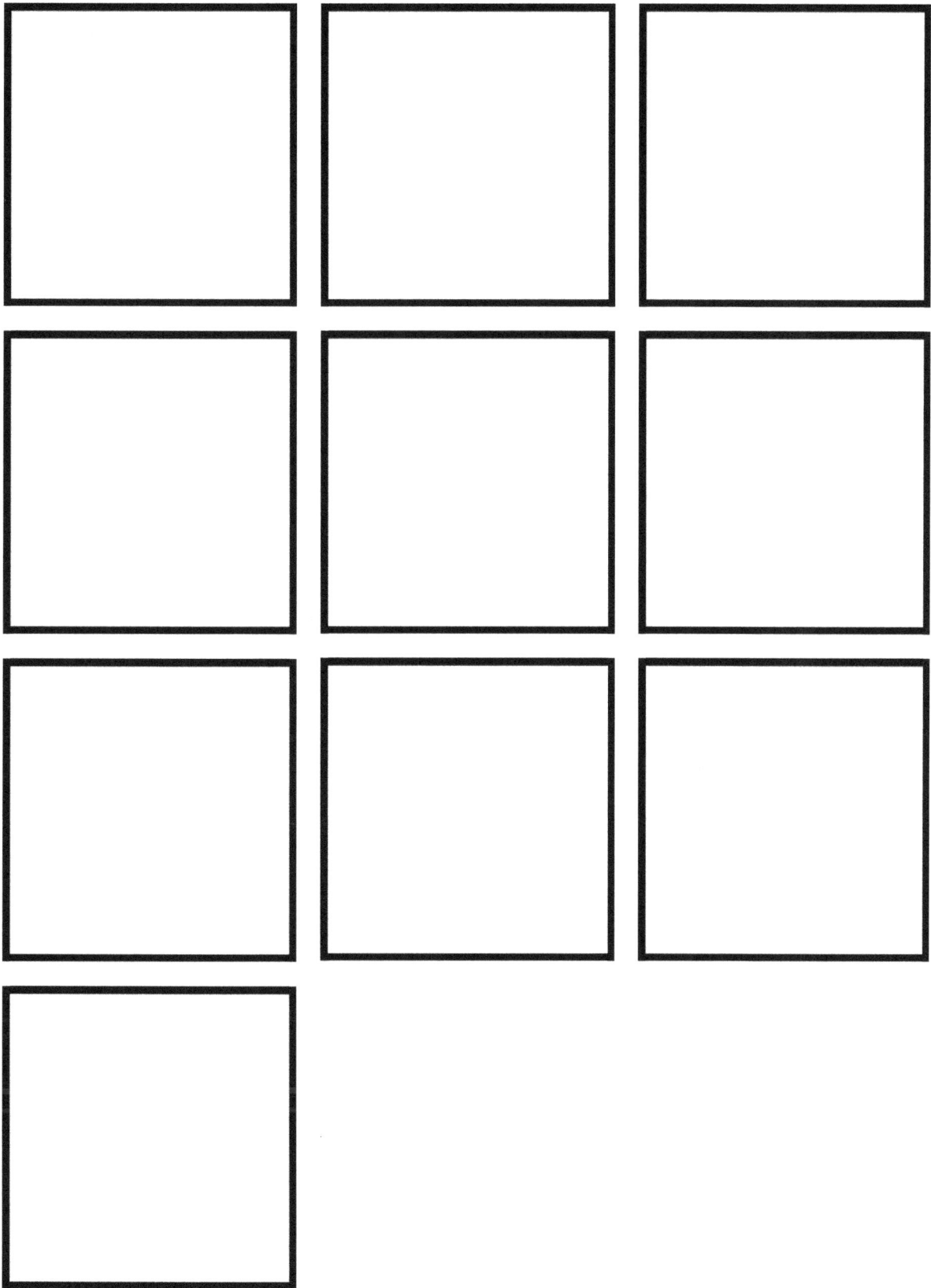

10 squares

www.ingramcontent.com/pod-product-compliance
Lightning Source LLC
Chambersburg PA
CBHW081218020426
42331CB00012B/3045